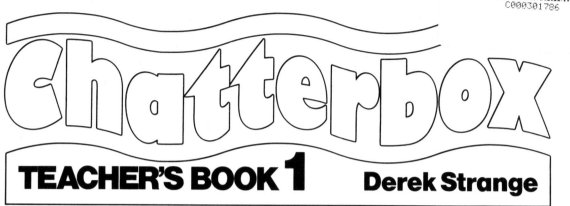

Chatterbox

TEACHER'S BOOK 1 — Derek Strange

Oxford University Press

Oxford University Press, Great Clarendon Street, Oxford OX2 6DP

Oxford New York
Auckland Bangkok Buenos Aires Cape Town Chennai
Dar es Salaam Delhi Hong Kong Istanbul Karachi Kolkata
Kuala Lumpur Madrid Melbourne Mexico City Mumbai
Nairobi São Paulo Shanghai Taipei Tokyo Toronto

OXFORD and OXFORD ENGLISH are trade marks of
Oxford University Press

ISBN 0 19 432433 8

© Derek Strange 1989

First published 1989
Fifteenth impression 2003

Set by Pentacor Ltd

Printed in Hong Kong

INTRODUCTION

General description of the course

Chatterbox is a four-level course for children of primary school age who are learning English for the first time. There are fifteen units in each level. A unit contains material for three lessons of 50 minutes each with additional material for extra work in class and for homework.

The components at each level are a Pupil's Book, an Activity Book, a Teacher's Book and a cassette.
At the back of this Teacher's Book are three Tests and a Handwriting Booklet.
The Pupil's Book presents new words, grammar structures and functions in imaginative and clear contexts. A continuing adventure story, featuring ace detective, Captain Shadow, and a variety of songs, rhymes and games are used to practise new language in an enjoyable way. The story, songs and various other listening activities are recorded on the Cassette.
The Activity Book consolidates the language points of the Pupil's Book with reading and writing exercises and puzzles, and can be used in class or for homework.
The Teacher's Book gives step-by-step lesson plans and answers, and extra ideas for classroom activities.

Aims and syllabus

The three main aims of *Chatterbox* are:
● to help pupils understand and use some basic structures of English grammar correctly in a variety of purposeful communicative activities.
● to help pupils develop confidence in listening, speaking, reading and writing in English, using a good basic range of vocabulary.
● to make learning English an enjoyable and meaningful experience through an exciting story, songs, rhymes, games and puzzles.

The syllabus of *Chatterbox* is based on graded structures and vocabulary. Language items have been chosen according to the criteria of frequency,

usefulness and simplicity, although some words are occasionally introduced which are specific to a particular story episode or topic. Each language item is recycled and revised regularly.
Closely linked to the structural syllabus is the syllabus of functions and topics, which covers areas of interest within the experience of children. Through interesting topics *Chatterbox* systematically develops pupils' motivation and skills in listening, speaking, reading and writing.

Characters in *Chatterbox*

The story episodes revolve round the adventures in London of a ten-year-old twin brother and sister, Poppy and Bean, and their nine-year-old friend Woody. They meet the famous detective, Captain Shadow, who has a large friendly dog called Pluto. Captain Shadow works in both London and New York. In the Level 1 story she is in London on the trail of Mr X, a bank robber, and his accomplice, Lifter.
Various other characters appear outside the story page of each unit. There is Zoko, the friendly robot, who is often accompanied by three friends - Kate, Ken and Caroline. And finally there is the green 'monster' family of Lucy, with her mother and father, two brothers, her little sister and aunts, uncles and cousins.

How to use the Course Books

Each unit of the Pupil's Book and the Activity Book is four pages long. One unit provides work for a minimum of three 50-minute lessons.

Lesson One

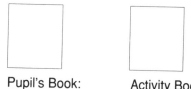

Pupil's Book: first page of the unit.

Activity Book: first page of the unit.

The first page of the Pupil's Book unit presents the main new structure and vocabulary for the unit, usually with an accompanying cassette section. The new language is then practised in class through oral drills and through a question and answer activity, usually introduced in the Pupil's Book by Zoko and one of his friends, shown as 'talking heads'. The talking heads give model questions and answers which pupils use to start talking about the pictures in the Pupil's Book.

What's this?

It's the big box.

The first page of the Activity Book unit contains follow-up reading and writing exercises to consolidate the new language.

Lesson Two

Pupil's Book:
second and third
pages of the unit.

Activity Book:
second page of
the unit.

The first part of this lesson is based on the Captain Shadow adventure story which appears on the second page of every Pupil's Book unit (except for the first unit in the book). Pupils listen to the cassette and read the story in their books. They then practise a short dialogue from the story which they may act out in class. The second part of the lesson is based on the third page of the Pupil's Book unit. This page often presents a new language item and usually contains an activity box called a 'Language puzzle', or a song or rhyme, to practise the new language.

This new language is consolidated in exercises on the second Activity Book page for the unit.

Lesson Three

Pupil's Book:
fourth page of
the unit.

Activity Book:
third and fourth
pages of the unit.

The third lesson provides opportunities for pupils to consolidate and extend their use of new language through a song or a game or a reading activity. The emphasis here is on using what pupils have already learnt in an enjoyable new way.

The corresponding pages of the Activity Book (pages 3 and 4 of the unit) consolidate the language pupils have learnt in that unit, usually ending with a word puzzle. From Unit 6 onwards the third page of the Activity Book unit includes a regular exercise on sounds and spellings in English.

Basic procedures - stages of the lesson

Revision/Warm-up
In the warm-up at the start of each lesson pupils use language they already know, often in an activity they have done before: a song or a short game. The warm-up should last for no more than five minutes.

Presentation
New language is sometimes first presented to pupils with their Pupil's Books closed, so that when they do open their books at the beginning of the unit some of the words and their meanings are already familiar and interesting language practice can begin more quickly and easily.

Presenting new language with 'books closed'.
New words and phrases are usually taught by showing real objects, by drawing simple pictures on the board, or by mime and gesture. Wherever possible, it is best to use real objects to present new words. Many of those presented in *Chatterbox* are for objects found in the classroom (e.g. furniture, clothing) or which can easily be brought into class (e.g. small toys). Only use the pupils' mother tongue to translate words when other methods of explanation are impossible.

Whenever a new word is introduced, make sure that pupils know how to pronounce it clearly. Use this procedure:
● Say the new word two or three times.
● Pupils listen and repeat the new word, first all together and then individually.

Presenting new language with 'books open'.
This method of presentation relies on the pictures on the Pupil's Book page and often on the cassette

recording that goes with it. There are three basic types of listening presentation which use the Pupil's Book and the cassette.

1 *Listen and repeat:* This procedure is used to present rhymes and other new language pupils can learn by heart.

2 *Listen and point ...* (or *Listen and match*):
● Pupils listen to the tape and look at the pictures on the page. They point to a particular picture or object which is named on the tape.
The *Listen and match* activities are a slightly more complex version of the *Listen and point* activities:
● Pupils listen to the tape and match each picture with a sentence or with another picture.

3 *Listen and read:* This procedure is used to present the story page.

Story presentation

● Before presenting a new episode of the story, summarize what has happened in the story so far by discussing it with pupils in their mother tongue. Ask them to tell you briefly what they remember about previous episodes.
Also before listening to the new story episode, pre-teach some of the new words which pupils will need to understand what happens. Use gesture and mime or board drawings to do this.
● Play the cassette section for the story episode right through once while pupils listen and read the speech bubbles.
● Play the story again. Pupils listen a second time and repeat the sentences after the recording for pronunciation and reading practice. In later episodes of the story this part of the procedure is replaced by a second *listen and read* stage in which pupils look for answers to pre-set questions.
● After listening to the story, go on to any further activities suggested in the notes.

Practice

Speaking and listening

Drills. The aim of speed drills is to help pupils learn the pronunciation and patterns of new language. They should be done at a rapid, lively pace.
● For new words: hold up or point to objects, pictures, etc. Pupils name them in chorus, then individually. Go faster and faster.
● For structures: say a cue-word or -phrase once or

twice. Pupils respond by giving a whole sentence, using the required structure. Again, keep up a rapid pace.

'Chain drills'. Use the following procedure:
● One pupil makes a statement to the next pupil, e.g. *Hello. My name's George. What's your name?* The next pupil replies *Hello. My name's Mary*, and then turns to a third pupil and says, *What's your name?* Pupils continue in this way round the class, each pupil in turn adding a new 'link' to the chain.

Question and answer practice. The *Ask and answer* sections in the Pupil's Book give opportunities for slightly less controlled practice based on the pictures on the Pupil's Book page. A model of the questions and answers needed to talk about the pictures is presented by the 'talking heads' of Zoko and another character.
● Begin by asking the questions yourself and helping pupils to reply.
● Gradually get pupils to take over the questioning so that they are asking and answering each other, looking at the pictures for their answers.

Pair work. Question and answer practice leads naturally on to pair work, where pupils ask and answer each other in pairs. Go round checking pupils' pronunciation and understanding.

Teacher questions and 'transfer'. In some lessons more 'open' and varied questions are suggested which can be used to ask pupils about what they can see in the pictures on the page or what they have read or heard. They can often also be developed to ask pupils about themselves, their own situation and experience - this *transfer* of question and answer practice to the pupils' own 'world' makes the use of English obviously meaningful for them and is strongly recommended wherever possible.

Dialogues. Dialogue or role play practice is based on short sections from the story episodes.
● Play the relevant part of the story on the cassette. Pupils listen and repeat each phrase first in chorus, then individually.
● Ask one pair of pupils to come out and demonstrate the dialogue together for the others.
● Pupils in pairs practise the dialogue, taking one part each.
● When they are ready, one or two pairs read and act out the dialogue for the rest of the class.

Reading

Chatterbox Level 1 has a strictly graded approach to reading so that pupils who are not familiar with the English alphabet or who have not been reading for very long in their mother tongue can cope easily. Pupils are first taught to recognize the letters of the alphabet and then whole words by the *Look and say* method. New reading vocabulary is presented largely through *listen and read* use of the story episodes where the meaning of words is clear from their context and is supported by the pictures. Recognition of new words and their spelling is reinforced through Activity Book exercises, and class games such as Alphabet Races, Bingo! etc. From Unit 6 of the Activity Book onwards, once a basic *look and say* reading vocabulary has been established in the first five units, pupils are helped to recognize relations between written letters and their spoken sounds (the 'phonics' of reading) in a special series of exercises. Some ability to decipher new words in this way will increase pupils' confidence in reading English.

In using the letters-and-sounds (phonics) exercises from Unit 6 of the Activity Book onwards, follow the procedure set out in the notes for each unit.

As pupils' abilities in reading English develop, so too do the variety of topics and the length of the reading passages in *Chatterbox*. Some of the texts are 'informational' (about places, people, etc.), some are 'comic-fictional' (e.g. 'Bob the Bad Banana') and some reading takes place in a specially designed reading game ('Shops: a reading game').
Exploit these reading pages in the Pupil's Book by using the following procedure:
● Before reading: pre-set any questions suggested in lesson notes.
● While reading: ask pupils to read silently on their own or aloud in turn round the class, or else to work out passages together in pairs. Choose the approach which best suits a particular class and their mood in a particular lesson.
Go round helping as necessary, but encourage pupils to develop the skill of guessing meanings of unknown words from their context or from clues in the pictures, and not to worry if they do not understand every word.
● After reading: check answers with the whole class, especially if a reading page has been completed for homework.

Writing

The Handwriting Booklet. This is for pupils whose mother tongue does not use the same script as English.

The sequencing of the letters presented and practised in the Handwriting Book is by their order of 'frequency' - by how often a particular letter actually occurs in written English. For example, the letter **e** actually occurs more frequently in written English than any other letter, with the letter **t** next, then **a**, then **o**, and so on. By introducing and practising letters according to this order of 'frequency', pupils immediately learn those letters they will need to read and write more often than others. In using the exercises in the Handwriting Booklet, follow this procedure:
● Draw six base lines on the board. Write the letters to be practised one by one on the lines and describe (in mother tongue) the hand movements you are making. Repeat each letter five or six times along the lines, describing the hand movements each time, and ensuring that pupils understand the relationship of each letter to the base line.

● When all the new letters in an exercise have been described and demonstrated in this way, pupils trace and then copy them (in pencil, to allow for corrections) on the guide-lines in each exercise.
● Handwriting exercises may be completed for homework once their aim is fully understood.

'Language puzzles' in the Pupil's Book. Most units in the Pupil's Book contain a *Language puzzle* which gives opportunities for further oral practice followed by controlled written practice of the main grammar points of the unit.
Punctuation can be taught and practised through the *Language puzzle* boxes also. In these boxes punctuation marks often appear as separate, meaningful components of sentence structures. In the teacher's notes for early lessons some specific reminders on teaching the form and function of English punctuation marks are also given. In all written work, encourage accuracy in punctuation.

Writing exercises in the Activity Book. Most writing practice, for consolidation of new grammar and vocabulary, takes place in the *Chatterbox* Activity Book. Exercises can be done either in class or for homework. Introduce Activity Book exercises in the following way:
● Go over one or two sentences from any written exercise orally first to ensure that all pupils understand the aim of the exercise and what they have to do. If the

exercise is done in class and not for homework, go round checking and helping with pupils' work.

Spelling. Practice in spelling takes place regularly through a variety of suggestions for extra word-games in class and through specific spelling exercises and word-puzzles in the Activity Book. Follow the suggestions for the individual exercises and games given in lesson notes.

Special procedures for specific activities

Songs and rhymes

The songs, rhymes and chants in *Chatterbox* have all been specially written to focus on specific points of grammar or areas of vocabulary. They are intended as fun, lively ways of presenting and then practising new language so that pupils can remember it more easily.
● Play the cassette section. Pupils first listen with books either open or closed, as you wish.
● Play the cassette once or twice more. Pupils *listen and sing* along with the song or recite the rhyme, following the words in their books.
● Encourage pupils to learn the songs and rhymes by heart for homework. Use them frequently for lesson 'warm-ups' or endings, as suggested.

Games

In games pupils are able to practise using their English in the context of lively, meaningful speaking and listening activities in which they can participate unself-consciously. A variety of easy-to-manage games are used in Level 1 of *Chatterbox*.

Class or Team games in *Chatterbox* include
- (Black)board races: see 'The Alphabet Race' (Unit 2, Lesson 1).
- Identification games: see 'Who's this?' (Unit 1, Lesson 3), 'Who am I?' (Unit 7, Lesson 3).
- Word games: see 'The Spelling Shark' (Unit 2, Lesson 3), Anagrams (Unit 8, Lesson 3 and Unit 9, Lesson 1), 'What can I see?' (Unit 9, Lesson 3).
- Listening games: the 'Please and Thank you' game (Unit 6, Lesson 2), the plural endings listening discrimination game (Unit 12, Lesson 2).
- Pronunciation games: Tongue-twisters (Unit 6, Lesson 3 etc.) - for practice of word stress and sentence rhythm patterns also.

Games for pairs in *Chatterbox* include
- Identification games: as described above.
- Reading games: see 'Shops: a reading game' (Unit 13, Lesson 3), 'A game: What's in your box?' (Unit 14, Lesson 3).

Games for individuals in *Chatterbox* include
- Vocabulary games: see Bingo! (Unit 5, Lesson 3 etc.)
- Word puzzles: crossword puzzles, word squares, letter chains, etc. in the Activity Book.

Before starting to play a class or team game, the following procedures are recommended:

1. Name teams. Divide the class into teams. Give each team an English name, e.g. the Lions and the Monkeys. Vary the team names lesson by lesson to practise new words. Write team names on the board for scoring during games.
2. Choose players. Use a 'choosing rhyme' such as the following, to add suspense and pupil-involvement to the process of picking players for class or team games:

Eeny, Meeny, Miney, Mo,
Choose a person; off we GO!

The pupil chosen is the one you are pointing at on the word *GO!*
● Always get pupils to chant with you.

Dictations

'Story-line' dictations. These can be based on small pieces of text from recent story episodes, as suggested in Unit 4, Lesson 3. Such 'auto-dictations' can be planned into any later lesson also, as necessary.
● Pupils try to fill in missing words from memory by saying the whole sentence to themselves.
● Alternatively, pupils can work together in pairs, agreeing on missing words, their spellings, etc.
● Pupils check their own dictation by looking back at the relevant section of the story.

Picture ('Picasso') dictations. These can be represented to pupils as 'drawing games':
● Pupils listen and draw in response to simple instructions. Give each instruction two or three times at near-normal speed and rhythm.
● Go over the 'dictation' by getting pupils to listen again and take turns to draw on the board.

Tests

The *Chatterbox* Tests at the back of this Teacher's Book provide a simple test of reading and writing skills for pupils to do after every fifth unit of the course. When setting a test

● Check that all pupils understand what they have to do. Go over the instruction and the example given for each section of the test and demonstrate what they should do.

● Pupils complete the test exercises one by one. Use the pupils' results to determine where further teaching and further practice may be necessary for the whole class or for individuals. Evaluation of pupils' skills in speaking and listening should be done on the basis of their regular participation in class.

Syllabus

Unit		Language items	Functions and topics
1	page 1	*Hello. Goodbye.* *What's your name?* *I'm . . .* *My name's Woody.* *Who's this? This is . . .* Possessives: *my/your.* The alphabet.	Greeting and saying farewell. Asking someone's name. Introducing yourself. Introducing others. Talking about possession.
2	page 5	*Listen, please.* *What's this?* Article: *a* + noun. *Good morning. How are you?* *I'm fine, thank you.*	Commands. Identifying things. Further greetings and responses.
3	page 9	Numbers 1–10. *How old are you? I'm ten.* *We're twins.* *This is 94312.* Article: *an* + a e i o u.	Counting. Talking about age. Telephone numbers.
4	page 13	*It's a kite.*	Naming common toys and household objects.
5	page 17	*He's seven. She's eight.* Possessives: *his/her.* Revision.	Talking about possession.
6	page 21	*Is it an aeroplane?* *Yes, it is./No, it isn't.* Article: *the* + noun. Adjectives: *the big/small box.*	Asking for information. Specifying particular objects.
7	page 25	*I've got a big nose.* *This is my mother.* *She's got big eyes.* *We've got a letter.*	Describing people: faces and hair. Members of the family.

Syllabus continued

Unit		Language items	Functions and topics
8	page 29	*Have you got your bag?* *Yes, I have./No, I haven't.* *Has she got her umbrella?* *Yes, she has./No, she hasn't.* Adjectives: *tall, short, etc.*	Asking for information. Describing people.
9	page 33	*Can you see an elephant?* *Yes, I can./No, I can't.* *Whose cage is this?* Possessive_'s: *the lion's cage.* *Turn right, turn left.*	Talking about ability. Talking about possession. Zoo animals. Giving directions.
10	page 37	*Show me the green kite.* *What colour is her skirt?* *It's red.* Revision.	Colours. Clothes.
11	page 41	*He's got brown legs.* *He's from England.*	Parts of the body. Saying where people or things come from.
12	page 45	Plural nouns: *–s/–es.* *There's . . ./There are . . .* *Is there . . . ?* *Yes, there is./No, there isn't.* Prepositions: *in, on.*	Describing situations. Asking for information. Specifying location.
13	page 49	*How many monsters are there?* *How many . . . can you see?* Preposition: *at + the bank, etc.*	Asking about number. Shops and places in town.
14	page 53	*What time is it?* *It's twelve o'clock.* *At eleven o'clock . . .* *. . . in the morning/evening.*	Asking and telling the time. Specifying the time of day.
15	page 57	*Square, circle, triangle.* Revision.	Talking about shape.

UNIT 1

Lesson One

Language focus

Greetings and introductions: *Hello. What's your name?*
I'm (Miss / Mrs / Mr) ... .

The verb *to be*: *am ('m) is ('s).*

Classroom English

Look! Listen! Open/Close your books, please. Good!
Sit down, please. Goodbye.

Presentation

1 Introduce yourself. Shake hands with pupils: *Hello,
I'm (Miss)... .* Pupils repeat together after you:
Hello, I'm... .

2 Ask *What's your name?* Pupils repeat the question
in chorus.

3 Ask individual pupils *What's your name?*
● Pair work (see Introduction, p.5): Pupils ask each
other their names.

Practice (PUPIL'S BOOK p.1 CS1*)

4 *What's your name?* Give instructions: *Open your
books, please. Look! Listen!* Show by gestures
what you mean.
● Play the first section of CS1. Pupils listen and
read PB p.1.Play the rest of CS1. Pupils listen and
repeat after each speaker.
● Teach the short form - long form linking of *'m* and
am, *'s* and *is*. Show on the board how the
apostrophe replaces letters in the shortened form:
I'm →I am   What's → What is. Teach the form,
position and meaning of the question mark at the
end of Zoko's question.

5 Play a quick listening game. Just say the name of
any of the characters on PB p.1 two or three times.
Pupils listen and point to the face of the character
named.

6   (Extra) Transfer (see Introduction, p.5): Choose a
pupil to come to the front of the class.
● Ask *What's your name?* After the pupil has replied,
say *Good!... Sit down please, (name).* Repeat with
two or three pupils, using the same language.
● Choose a pupil to take the part of 'teacher',
asking *What's your name?*

Reading (ACTIVITY BOOK p.1)

7 **Activity ①** Pupils match the faces with the names
by drawing lines, as in the example.

Answers   Hello, I'm Poppy.
                Hello, I'm Bean.
                Hello, I'm Zoko.

Ending the lesson

8 Say *Close your books, please.* Then say *Goodbye!*
several times.Pupils repeat after you two or three
times. Make sure that they understand the
difference between *Hello* (when you meet) and
Goodbye (when you leave).
● Say *Goodbye* to individual pupils as they leave
the class.

Be prepared!

Ask pupils to bring one plain rectangular sheet of
paper with them, folded longways down the centre,
for use in Lesson 2, or have one ready for each
child.

Lesson Two

Language focus
The alphabet: small letters.
Who's this? This is (Poppy).

Classroom English
*Come in, please. Well done! Everyone, please.
Together, please.*

Revision/Warm-up

1 Greet pupils as they arrive and settle down:
Come in, please. Sit down, please.
● Say *Hello, I'm (Miss)...* two or three times,
pointing at yourself. Ask some pupils *What's
your name?* Write up the (ten or so) names at
random on the board as they tell you.
● Pair work: Pupils introduce themselves to their
neighbours in the same way.

2 │ (Extra) 'Name labels': Pupils have one sheet of plain
│ paper each. Get them to fold it in half down the
│ centre and draw a base line to write on, near the
│ bottom of one side.
│ ● Finish writing up all the pupils' names at random
│ on the board.
│ ● Read the names on the board one by one. Pupils
│ repeat after you (say *Everyone, please*). Pupils copy
│ their own name onto their paper. Go round helping
│ and praising them by saying *Good.*

Song presentation (PUPIL'S BOOK p.2 CS2)

3 *a...b...c...d...* (see Introduction, p.7) 'Songs and
Rhymes'):Pupils listen once to the song with books
closed.
● They then open their books at PB p.2 and listen
again, trying to sing along.

Story presentation (PUPIL'S BOOK p.3 CS3)

4 *This is Woody.* Context: Poppy and Bean are at an
adventure playground. They make a new friend
there, called Woody.
● Say *Look! Listen!* Play CS3. Pupils listen and
read.
● Play CS3 again: Pupils listen and repeat together
after each speaker.
[NOTE: It can be beneficial to invite pupils' parents
to take an interest in the development of the story
week by week. Pupils can retell story episodes to their
parents in their own language.]

Story practice

5 Dialogue (see Introduction, p.5). Pupils read and
practise **Pictures 3 and 4 only,** as a short two-part
dialogue, first as a class and then in pairs. Build up
the dialogue with the 'chain drills' procedure, if
necessary (see Introduction,p.5). Go round helping
in the pair work stage.
● One or two pairs come up and act out the
dialogue. Praise their efforts: *Good! Well done!*

6 Transfer : Ask pupils to identify each other by
asking *Who's this?* and helping them to answer
This is... .

Reading and writing

(ACTIVITY BOOK pp. 1 - 2)

7 AB p.1 **Activity ②** Pupils draw a 'portrait' of
themselves in the frame. They then complete the
speech bubble by writing in their own name. Go
round helping where necessary.

8 AB p.2 **Activity ③** Pupils find and circle the
names of Poppy, Bean, Woody and Zoko, which are
hidden in the picture.

Answers

9 AB p.2 **Activity ④** Pupils write in the missing
letters in the names of the four characters.

Ending the lesson

10 As for Lesson 1.

Be prepared!

Bring a large handkerchief or scarf to the next
lesson to use as a blindfold.

Lesson Three

Language focus
Yes/No

Classroom English
Stand up, please. Stop!

Revision/Warm-up

1 Revise greetings and introductions with some pupils: *Hello, I'm... .What's your name?*

Presentation

2 Pre-teach *Yes* and *No* with typical head movements. Show pupils what the English head movements for *Yes* and *No* are, if necessary. Drill these a few times with the new words and head movements together.
● Ask pupils to put their name labels in front of them, but **facing towards them.**
● Go round asking aloud *Who's this?* and then trying to guess pupils' names without seeing their labels *(This is...)*. Pupils respond *Yes* or *No* to your guesses.
● Individual pupils come out and try to name all the other pupils from memory *(This is...)*. (Pupils should put up their labels in front of them from now on.)

Practice (PUPIL'S BOOK p.4)

3 PB p.4 *Who's this?* Pupils in turn name the characters shown in the pictures: *a. This is...* etc. The other pupils listen and agree *(Yes. Well done.)* or disagree and correct *(No. This is...)*.

Answers   a Poppy   c Woody
              b Bean   d Zoko

4 PB p.4 *A Game* (see Introduction, p.7 'Choose players'): Read aloud the game panel. Point out the words *Yes* and *Well done!* which pupils will not have come across in writing before.
● One pupil is then chosen to be blindfolded with a handkerchief or scarf, as shown in the picture. Other pupils then take turns to say *Hello...*, and the blindfolded player tries to guess from the voice who is speaking. Ken and Kate are characters who will reappear throughout this book, so they could be introduced to pupils here: *This is Ken ... This is Kate.* They will be formally introduced in Unit 5.

Reading (ACTIVITY BOOK pp. 3-4)

5 AB p.3 **Activity** ⑤ Pupils complete the dot-to-dot pictures of the PB characters and then match each

picture to the right name.

6 AB p.4 **Activity** ⑥ Pupils read the words in the box at the top and then find and circle the same words hidden in the letter square.

Answers

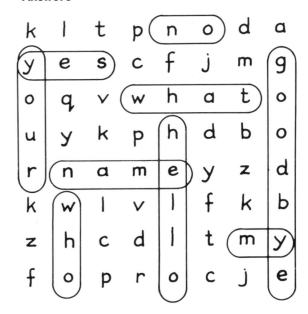

Ending the lesson

7 If there is time, sing the Alphabet Song (*a... b... c... d...*) again.

[NOTE: Use the same Starting and Ending lesson routines from now on, gradually expanding and varying them as the pupils' English develops.]

UNIT 2

Lesson One

Language focus
Commands: *Listen. Look.* etc.

Classroom English
Quiet, please. Stand up, please. Repeat, please.

Revision/Warm-up

1 Sing the Alphabet Song with CS2, if necessary.

Presentation (PUPIL'S BOOK p.5, CS4)

2 Books closed. Demonstrate basic classroom instructions by telling a pupil what to do and showing what you mean with clear mimed actions repeated two or three times. Say each instruction several times as the pupil responds to it. The other pupils listen and repeat (*Repeat, please.*):
T: *Come in... Stop!... Quiet, please... Listen... Sit down, please... Stand up, please... etc.*

3 PB p.5 CS4. *Listen please:* Play CS4. Pupils listen and look at their books.
   ● Play CS4 again. Pupils listen and point to the right picture, identifying each one by its letter.

Answers

Listen (picture a)   Come in (picture c)
Stop (picture d)   Quiet, please (picture f)
Look (picture b)   Sit down, please (picture e)

Practice

4 Pair work: Call out the commands in random order again, but faster this time. Pupils listen and point to the right picture.
   ● Ask one pupil to call out the commands in the same way, while the others listen and point.
   ● Put pupils into pairs now. Ask one pair to demonstrate the pair work activity: they take turns to give instructions from the top of PB p.5, and their partner names pictures by the appropriate letters.

5 PB p.5 *A Game:* The pictures in the book show how the game is played. Pupils are chosen in turns to come out and give various instructions to other pupils in the class, who must react with the right actions.
   ● Point out the words *Sit down..., Stand up...* and *please* which pupils have not met in writing before.

Reading (ACTIVITY BOOK p.5)

6 **Activity ①** Read through the speech bubbles one by one. Pupils listen and follow in their books. They have not met the words *Stop* or *No* in writing before, so point them out specifically here.
   ● Pupils then read and match the six speech bubbles with the six pictures.

Answers   1. Look.   4. No.
                 2. Yes.   5. Goodbye.
                 3. Listen.   6. Stop.

Ending the lesson

7   Alphabet Race: Divide the class into two teams (see Introduction, p.7 'Naming teams'). Write the small letters of the alphabet at random across the board as the class chant out the alphabet all together:

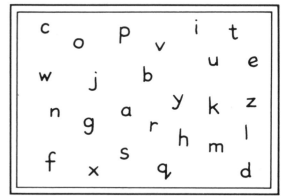

   ● Call out one player from each team. Give some chalk to each one. Explain that they are going to have an 'Alphabet Race'.
   ● Call out any letter of the alphabet, in random order. The two players race to find it on the board. One team puts crosses (X) through letters if they find them first, and the other team puts circles round letters (0). After every two or three letters, two new players come out and take over the race.
   ● Have two or three races, if there is time.

Be prepared!

Bring a soft cloth bag, or plastic bag one cannot see through to the next lesson (i.e. the Feelie Bag). You will also need a pen, a pencil, a small ruler, a rubber, a cassette and a small book (e.g. a phrase book) as similar as possible in size to the cassette.

Lesson Two

Language focus

Good morning!　Good afternoon!　How are you today?
I'm fine, thank you.　What's this?　The indefinite article: *a*

New words

a pencil　a pen　a ruler　a bag　a rubber　a desk　a table
a book.

Revision/Warm-up

1　Chain game (see Introduction, p.5 'Chain drills'):
Start an introductions chain round the class, like
this:

T to Pupil 1:	*Hello, my name's Miss... .*
	What's your name?
Pupil 1 to T:	*My name's George.*
Pupil 1 to Pupil 2:	*Hello, my name's George.*
	What's your name?
Pupil 2 :	*My name's Mary.*

Pupil 2 continues by asking Pupil 3 the question
and so on, round the class.

Story presentation (PUPIL'S BOOK p.6 CS5)

2　*Good morning!* Context: Captain Shadow, the
detective, Pluto her dog, and Luke her computer are
introduced in this episode.
● Before listening: Pre-teach *Good morning* (and
Good afternoon for use in afternoon classes). Also
teach the exchange *How are you today?... I'm fine,
thank you.* Teach and practise the question *How are
you?* first. Then get pupils to ask **you** *How are you
today?* so that you can introduce and practise the
answer *I'm fine... .* Practise this short exchange of
greetings with individual pupils round the class.
● Play CS5. Pupils listen and read.
● Play CS5 again. Pupils listen and repeat, first
together and then individually.
● After listening: Teach the word *Here!* for giving
something to someone, and the polite response
Thank you. Demonstrate its use by giving small
objects to members of the class, and helping them
to say *Thank you.*

Story practice

3　Dialogue: Pupils in pairs read and practise **Picture
1 only.** Use 'chaining' to drill and build up the
dialogue with the whole class first, if necessary.
● One or two pairs act out the dialogue.

Presentation (PUPIL'S BOOK p.7)

4　Books closed. The Feelie Bag. Put the small
classroom objects listed above (pen, pencil, ruler,
rubber, cassette, small book, etc.) one by one into
the Feelie Bag, naming each one clearly twice as
you put it in.
● Put your hand in the bag, feel, ask *What's this?*
several times (looking puzzled). Then pull out the
objects one by one.Name each object two or three
times again after pulling it out: *a ruler... a ruler... .*
● Pupils repeat the name of each object after you.
● Present and practise *a table*, *a desk* and *a book*,
pointing at and naming the objects. Pupils listen
and repeat.

Practice

5　'Speed drill' the new words (see Introduction, p.5).
Gradually point faster and faster at the objects
named and drilled.
6　Choose a pupil to come out, feel in the bag and ask
What's this?, keeping the object hidden in the bag.
The other pupils try to guess (e.g. *a rubber?...
a pencil?*).
● Do the same thing with different pupils.
7　PB p.7 *What's this?*: Read out the newly introduced
words at the top of the page. Pupils listen, read and
repeat. 'Look and say' reading practice of this kind is
the basis of the early part of the *Chatterbox* reading
programme (see Introduction, p.6).Ask *What's this?*
about one or two of the photographs below:
T: *(Pointing at **a**) What's this?*　　P: *A cassette.*
8　Pair work: Pupils take turns to ask about and identify
the photos in the same way. Go round helping with
pronunciation.

Answers	a. a cassette	d. a pen	g. a table
	b. a ruler	e. a bag	h. a rubber
	c. a book	f. a pencil	i. a cassette

Reading (ACTIVITY BOOK p.6)

9　**Activity ②**　Pupils read the words at the top and
match each one with one of the pictures below.
They write the letter of each picture in the
appropriate box.

| **Answers** | 1. c | 3. b | 5. g | 7. a |
| | 2. e | 4. h | 6. f | 8. d |

Ending the lesson

10　Repeat the Alphabet Race, if there is time (see
Lesson1).

Lesson Three

Language focus
Revision of *Hello*, *Goodbye*, etc.

Revision/Warm-up

1 Play the 'Who's this?' blindfold game to revise *This is...* (see PB p.4). Play the game twice.

Song presentation (PUPIL'S BOOK p.8 CS6)

2 *How are you*? Before listening: Remind pupils of the different greetings for the different times of the day, *Good morning* and *Good afternoon*.
● Play CS6. Pupils listen to the new song.
● Play CS6 again. Pupils listen and try to sing along with the recording.

Practice (PUPIL'S BOOK p.8)

3 *Language puzzle*. Pupils read the first word or two of the split sentences on the left and try to match them with the correct endings on the right.

Answers

a. Good morning.   d. I'm fine, thanks.

b. How are you?   e. Here!... Thank you.

c. Fine, thank you.

Reading and writing

(ACTIVITY BOOK pp. 7-8)

4 p.7 **Activity** ③ Pupils read the speech bubbles and write in the missing words.

Answers

1. [Luke] Good *morning*, Captain!...
   [Captain Shadow] Good *morning*, Luke.

2. [Luke] How *are* you today?
   [Captain Shadow] I'm *fine*, thank you.

3. [Captain Shadow] Come *in*, Pluto.
   Thank *you*, Pluto.

4. [Captain Shadow] Goodbye, Luke!
   [Luke] *Goodbye*, Captain.

5 p.8 **Activity** ④ Pupils complete the crossword.
Answers

Ending the lesson

6 (Extra) The Spelling Shark: [This is a version of the traditional 'Hangman' game.] Briefly explain the stages of the game to the class, as outlined below:
● Think of any pupil's name (e.g. Woody). Don't say it aloud.
● Write up *two* sets of blank dashes for the letters in the name.
● Draw a 'cliff' line down from the end of the bottom row of blanks. At the bottom of the cliff is the sea and the shark.
● Pupils take turns to guess one letter in the name. If that letter *is* in the name, write it in the appropriate blank on the top row. If it is *not* in the name, draw a little 'stick figure' starting to walk along the bottom row of blanks towards the edge of the cliff. Pupils must guess all the letters correctly before the stick figure falls over the cliff and into the shark's jaws.
● Play two or three rounds with pupils' own names.

[NOTE: The Spelling Shark is a very good way to revise the spelling of any new vocabulary introduced from now on.]

Be prepared!

Bring ten of each of the following to the next lesson in the Feelie Bag: ten coins, ten matches, ten marbles, ten pens, ten peanuts, ten sweets, etc.

UNIT 3

Lesson One

Language focus
Numbers 0-10

Classroom English
Again!

New words
number

Revision/Warm-up

1 The 'Please and Thank you' game: Tell pupils to listen carefully and follow the instructions you give **only** when you say *Please*.
● Give a series of instructions in English, sometimes using *please* and sometimes not: *Stand up, please,... Sit down,... Sit down, please,...* etc.
● Pupils who respond to the instructions when you have **not** said *please* are out.

Presentation (PUPIL'S BOOK p.9 CS7)

2 Books closed. Count out loud ten pupils in the room. Do the same with ten books. Count them out loud onto the table: T: *One...two... three...* etc.
● In the Feelie Bag you should have ten coins, ten matches, ten marbles, ten pens, ten peanuts, ten sweets, etc. Pour them all out of the bag onto the desk in a pile. Then count them out loud into separate groups of ten on the desk.
● Pupils listen and repeat together after you each time.

3 Write the figures (not the words) 1-10 on the board with pupils chanting together as you write.
● Ask individuals to say the numbers in sequence as you point at each figure in turn. Teach the word *number* now by saying it as you point to each figure on the board: *Number one... number two... number three...* etc.

4 PB p.9 *Numbers*. Count through the balloons across the top, pointing at each in turn. Pupils are now meeting the words for the numbers for the first time.
● 'Speed drill' the numbers in the balloons by pointing faster and faster in sequence each time.

5 PB p.9 CS7. *Numbers* (see Introduction, p.7) 'Songs and Rhymes').Pupils listen and read.
● Play CS7 two or three times.

● Pupils join in as much as they can, clapping with the rhythm. Go through the rhyme several times without the tape. Introduce the instruction *Again, please* for the repeats.

Practice

6 Use the Feelie Bag again. Put back into the bag three or four pens (or whatever small object you prefer). Give the bag to a pupil. The pupil opens the bag and counts out the objects onto his or her desk.
● Choose a pupil to take the part of 'teacher', selecting a different number of the different sets of small objects to put into the bag each time.

7 (Extra) Adding game: Give examples of simple mental additions: *Two and four is... six; three and five is... eight*, etc. Make sure that pupils understand the new word *and* for addition here, by writing the sums in figures on the board (2 + 4 = 6, etc).
● Set simple mental additions for pupils to work out, for example,*What is four and three? What is seven and two?What is one and five?What is eight and two? What is six and four?* etc.
● Let pupils take over as 'teacher' as soon as possible.

Reading and writing (ACTIVITY BOOK p.9)

8 **Activity** ①Teach the number *zero*. Write the figure and the word for it on the board and say *This is zero... zero*. Pupils repeat the new number.
● Pupils read the words for the numbers in the rocket and match them with the figures in the stars by drawing lines.

9 **Activity** ②Pupils count the number of rockets and then write the word for that number.

Answers	a. one	c. six	e. two
	b. three	d. four	f. seven

Ending the lesson

10 Chant the Numbers Rhyme all together two or three times.

Lesson Two

Language focus
Indefinite article: *an*. *How old are you? I'm (ten).*
We are ('re).

Classroom English
Find...

New words
an apple   an elephant an icecream an orange
an umbrella twins

Revision/Warm-up

1 Chant the Numbers Rhyme all together, using CS7
again if necessary.

Story presentation (PUPIL'S BOOK p.10 CS8)

2 *How old are you?* Context: Poppy and Bean are
with their new friend, Woody. It is their birthday
today and they are looking at their birthday cards
with him.
● Before listening: Pre-teach the new word *twins*,
using Poppy and Bean, for example, *Poppy is ten
and Bean is ten, Poppy and Bean are twins.*
● Play CS8. Pupils listen and read. Pupils repeat,
first together and then individually.
● After listening: Write up the question *How old are
you?* Drill it by asking the question to one or two
pupils and helping them to answer *I'm (eight)*.
● Also teach the form and meaning of *We're → We
are*, as shown in Picture 4. Use a board sketch
again to demonstrate the function of the apostrophe,
as before.

Story practice

3 Dialogue: Pupils in pairs read and practise **Picture 3
only.** Drill and build up the dialogue with the whole
class first if necessary. Go round helping with
pronunciation and intonation during the pair work
stage.
● One or two pairs act out the dialogue.

4 Transfer: Ask about pupils' ages: *How old are **you**?*
(pointing at individual pupils in turn). Help pupils to
give full answers: *I'm...* .
● Find two pupils the same age. Ask the same
question as you point at them both. Help them to
answer together *We're (ten)*. Do the same with other
pairs of pupils.

Presentation (PUPIL'S BOOK p.11)

5 *An apple, an icecream* . Read the new words and
point to the pictures at the top of the page. Pupils
listen, read and repeat.
● Point out that *an* is used instead of *a* before
nouns beginning with vowels: *a, e, i, o, u.*
● Drill the new words with *an* two or three times
each.

Practice (PUPIL'S BOOK p.11)

6 Pupils look at the picture puzzle of the fairground.
The picture contains these hidden objects: an apple,
a bag, a ball, a boat, a book, an elephant,
an icecream, a pen, an umbrella. Pupils respond to
commands: T: *Find... an elephant. Find... a ball.
Find... an icecream. Find... a pen,* etc. Make sure
pupils understand the new instruction *Find...*
● Pair work: Pupils take turns to give each other
similar instructions, trying to find all the hidden
objects in the picture puzzle. Go round helping with
pronunciation.

7 *Language puzzle.* Pupils read each question and
decide which of the two indefinite articles in the
answer is the right one. If extra practice is required,
set some similar sentences on the board.
Answers　　1. an　2. a　　3. a

Reading and writing (ACTIVITY BOOK p.10)

8 **Activity ③** Pupils read each word and write *a* or *an*
in front of the word as appropriate.

Answers　　1. an apple　　6. a ruler
　　　　　　　　2. a book　　　7. an orange
　　　　　　　　3. an umbrella　8. an elephant
　　　　　　　　4. a bag　　　　9. a rubber
　　　　　　　　5. a cassette　　10. an icecream

Ending the lesson

9 Have a Numbers Race with numbers 0-10 on the
board (similar to the Alphabet Race of the previous
unit, page 14).

10　(Extra) Revision game: Partly hide any small **known**
object (e.g. a rubber, a short pencil, a pen, a
cassette, etc.) in your pocket or under a book or in
your hand. Pupils try to guess what it is:

T: *What's this?*　　P: *A ruler?*
T: *No.*　　　　　　P: *A pen?*
T: *Yes. Well done!*

● Choose pupils to come out in turn and face the
board with their hands held out behind their back.
Place an object in their hands. They then guess
what it is: *It's a ...* .

Lesson Three

Language focus
Telephone numbers: *This is 85791.*

New words
telephone

Revision/Warm-up

1 Draw a simple outline of any known object (taken from PB p. 7 and p.11) on the board and ask *What's this?* Pupils answer. Let pupils take over as 'teacher' if possible.

2 Speed drill the nouns pupils now know. Say the noun only and point at a pupil who should repeat the noun with its correct indefinite article:

T: *cassette*

P: *a cassette*

T: *orange*

P: *an orange* etc.

Presentation (PUPIL'S BOOK p.12)

3 Books closed. Teach the use of 'strings' of single numbers in telephone numbers and teach the new word *telephone* with a board drawing or a mime. Give your own telephone number: *My telephone number is... .*
[Note: '0' is given as *zero* and not *Oh* here to avoid confusion of the alphabet and numbers.]
● Ask pupils *What's your telephone number?* and help them to give answers correctly in English.
● Show pupils how to answer a phone call: mime answering the telephone and say *Hello? This is (your number).*
● Get pupils in turn to imitate the mime, giving their own telephone numbers: *Hello? This is (pupil's number).*

Practice (PUPIL'S BOOK p.12 CS9)

4 *Phone numbers.* Pupils take turns to look at the phone numbers given at the top and say them out loud. Remember: *0* is *zero.*

5 PB p.12 CS9 *Hello? This is 94312* . Play CS9 once through. Pupils listen.
● Play CS9 again, pausing after each speaker to give pupils time to find the phone number given by the speaker in each case.

Answers	1. 94312	3. 90632
	2. 75408	4. 75868

Reading and writing

(ACTIVITY BOOK pp.11-12)

6 AB p.11 **Activity** ④ Pupils write the words for the numbers shown round the telephone dial.

7 AB p.11 **Activity** ⑤ Pair work: Pupils take turns to read out the simple additions to their partner who works out the answer in English. Pupils then all write answers to the sums, in words.

Answers	1. nine	5. ten
	2. seven	6. five
	3. eight	7. six
	4. four	8. three

8 AB p.12 **Activity** ⑥ Pupils complete the sentences in the speech bubbles by choosing and writing in one of the words from the box in the middle.

Answers	1. What's *your* name?
	My *name* is Woody.
	2. What's *this*?
	An *umbrella*.
	3. How *are* you today?
	I'm fine, thank *you*.
	4. Hello? This *is* 94312.
	5. How *old* are you?
	I'm nine.

Ending the lesson

9 Play one or two rounds of the Spelling Shark (see page 16) using the number-words between *zero* and *ten.*

UNIT 4

Lesson One

Language focus
Identifying common toys and household objects:
It's a/an... .

Classroom English
Show me..., please.

New words
*an aeroplane a ball a balloon a bicycle a boat a car
a computer a doll a football   a kite Happy birthday!*

Revision/Warm-up

1 Counting Chain Game. Start a counting chain: the
first pupil in the chain says *Zero*, the next pupil *One*,
the next pupil *Two*, and so on. After *Ten*, go back to
Zero again. Any pupil who hesitates or says the
wrong number is 'out'. The last two or three pupils to
remain 'in' are the winners.

Presentation (PUPIL'S BOOK p.13)

2 *Happy birthday!* Teach the greeting *Happy
birthday!* and explain that it is Poppy's and Bean's
birthday today.
  ● To teach the new words on this page, tell pupils
to 'Listen and look!' Say each word two or three
times, pointing at the picture on the page:
aeroplane... aeroplane. Pupils listen and repeat.
Build up to the full sentence each time: *an
aeroplane... It's a/an... .* Pupils repeat the full
sentence after you.
  ● Drill pronunciation of all the new words again at
random, getting pupils to expand each one into a
short sentence with *It's... .*

Practice (PUPIL'S BOOK p.13 CS10)

3 *Happy birthday!* Play CS10. Pupils listen to the toy
named on the tape and find and point to it among all
the presents.

Tapescript

Voice 1:   Listen, look and point.

Ken: an aeroplane . . . . .
       a balloon . . . .
       a bicycle . . . .
       a ball . . . .

       a boat . . . .
       a car . . . .
       a computer . . . . . .
       a doll . . . .
       a football . . . .
       a kite . . . .

  ● Play CS10 again for pupils to listen and point
again, trying to spot the toys more quickly.

4 Pair work: Pupils take turns to point at any toy at
random on the page and ask *What's this?* Their
partner answers by identifying the toy by name: *It's
a/an... .*

5 | (Extra) The 'Please and Thank you' Game (see
page 17): Pre-teach *Show me a/an...* by mime
and gestures. Remind pupils that, in this game,
they should only do what you ask if you say
please - otherwise they should not respond.
● Say *Show me a...* for the pictures on PB
p.13, with and occasionally without the word
please. When pupils react correctly say *well
done!* and *thank you.*
● Let pupils take over as 'teacher' as soon as
possible.

Reading (ACTIVITY BOOK p.13)

6 **Activity ①** Pupils match the sentences with the
pictures and write in the identification letter of each
picture in the appropriate box.

Answers   1. b   5. d
             2. g   6. c
             3. a   7. e
             4. f   8. h

Ending the lesson

7 Game: Numbers Bingo! Pupils draw a six-square
bingo frame and write in each square of their frame
a different number between *zero* and *ten*. They
cross off each number as it is called out.

Be prepared!

Wrap two or three apples, oranges and small balls
in paper bags or in newspaper for the next lesson.

Lesson Two

Language focus
Identifying a person: *It's Woody.*

Classroom English
Guess!

New words
party thanks

Revision/Warm-up

1 Game: 'Guess!' Build up any of the pictures below, adding one new line at a time. After adding each new line, ask *What's this?* and say *Guess!* until pupils guess correctly. Complete the drawing and say *Yes. Well done. It's a/an... .*

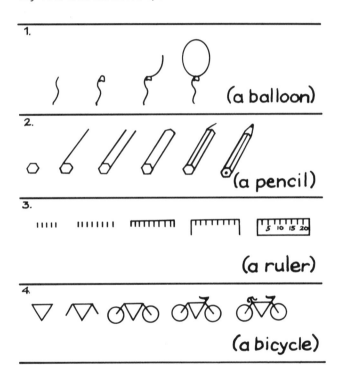

1.

(a balloon)

2.

(a pencil)

3.

(a ruler)

4.

(a bicycle)

Story presentation

(PUPIL'S BOOK p.14 CS11)

2 *It's a balloon.* Context: Bean and Poppy are having a birthday party with some of their friends. Woody is just arriving with his present for them... .
● Before listening: Pre-teach the word *party* by pointing to the first picture on p.14. Also teach *thanks* as the shortened informal form of *thank you*.
● Play CS11. Pupils listen and read.
● Play CS11 again. Pupils listen and repeat.

Story practice

3 Dialogue: Pupils in pairs practise **Pictures 3 and 5 together only.** Go round listening and helping.
● One or two pairs act out the dialogue.

Presentation (PUPIL'S BOOK p.15)

4 *A game: What's this?* Talk about the picture with pupils: the children at the birthday party are playing a guessing game. Poppy is holding a present and the others are guessing what it is.
● Put the wrapped balls, oranges and apples that you have brought in (all similar in shape, so that the guessing is real) on the desk.
● Hold one up and ask pupils: *What's this? Guess!* Let them take turns to come and feel each wrapped object before they try to guess what it is: *It's a/an... .*
● Let pupils take over and run the game as soon as possible.
● Remind pupils now of the short form - long form link between ' *s* and *is*. Repeat the Unit 1 board demonstration of the way the apostrophe replaces letters in the shortened form, if necessary.

My name's... → *My name is...*
What's this? → *What is this?*

Practice (PUPIL'S BOOK, p.15)

5 *Language puzzle*: Pupils follow the example, making properly ordered sentences from the jumbled words in the boxes.
● Make sure that pupils understand that a sentence begins with a capital letter and ends with a full stop (or a question mark if the sentence is a question).

Answers	1. What's this?	3. It's a ball.
	2. It's an orange.	4. Who's this?

Song presentation

(PUPIL'S BOOK p.15 CS12)

6 *Happy birthday to you!* Play CS12 right through. Pupils listen and follow in their books.
● Play CS12 again. Pupils listen and sing along.
● Play CS12 again if pupils wish.
[Note: If children usually celebrate their name day instead of their birthday, then change the words of the song to 'Happy name day...'. Explain that English children celebrate their birthday, not their name day. Sing the Happy Birthday song whenever a pupil has a

birthday that day. Find out and note all pupils' birthdays for this purpose.]

Writing (ACTIVITY BOOK p.14)

7 **Activity** ② Pupils follow the tangled lines from the pictures on the left and complete the sentences appropriately. Check they use the correct article (*a* or *an*) before the noun.

Answers	1. It's a kite.	4. It's a boat.
	2. It's an icecream.	5. It's a balloon.
	3. It's an aeroplane.	6. It's a ball.

Ending the lesson

8 Play a few rounds of Numbers Bingo! (see end of Lesson 1, p.20).

Be prepared!

Bring the Feelie Bag and different, known small objects to the next lesson.
Also bring in an unused envelope.

Lesson Three

Language focus
Revision of vocabulary

Revision/Warm-up

1 Game. Use The Feelie Bag again - this time with only one small toy or classroom object inside the bag each time. Pupils pass the closed bag round from one to another and they all, in turn, feel the object inside it.
● Meanwhile, write up two possibilities on the board, for example,
a. *It's a rubber.*   b. *It's a ball.*
When they have all felt the object inside the bag, pupils silently choose the sentence they think is true and copy it out.
● Change the object in the bag and play the game again in the same way.
● Check pupils' guesses by asking individuals to read back their sentences.

Presentation (PUPIL'S BOOK p.16)

2 *A game: Listen and find* . Pre-teach the word *envelope* by showing pupils the one you have brought into class. Drill the pronunciation of the new word.
● Ask pupils to look at the picture on p.16 and point to the things you name:*Find a computer... Find an umbrella...* etc. Then show them how each of the objects is in one square of the grid drawn over the picture. Name more objects and ask pupils to identify which squares they are in, naming the square by its letter (across the top) and its number (downwards). Zoko and Kate are playing this game at the top of the page.

Practice

3 Pair work: Pupils play the game, taking turns to name an object on the page and turns to find it.

4 | (Extra) Dictation: Write up Woody's words from the recent story episode on the board, leaving three gaps:
It's _ _ _ balloon, a _ _ _ _ _ for your _ _ _ _ _.
● Pupils have to try to fill in the missing words from memory, by 'auto-dictation', without looking back at the relevant page. Go round helping with spellings, as necessary.
● Pupils look back at PB p.14 and check their own dictations against the original.

Reading and writing

(ACTIVITY BOOK pp.15-16)

5 AB p.15 **Activity** ③ Pupils write *my* or *your* in the gaps in the speech bubbles.

Answers   1. my   3. your   5. your
              2. my   4. your   6. my

6 AB p.16 **Activity** ④ Write up and read out the word *envelope* several times to ensure pupils are able to recognize it in its written form.
   ● Pupils then isolate and circle the individual words which are in the 'word chain'. They link each word to its corresponding picture.
   Answers. The words are, in order: *umbrella, aeroplane, envelope, elephant, table.*

7 AB p.16 **Activity** ⑤ Pupils find and circle the words hidden in the letter square.

Answers

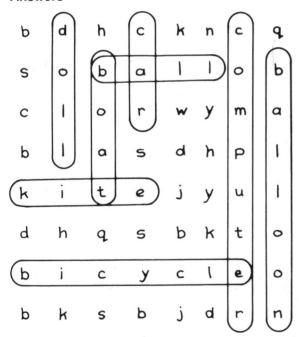

Ending the lesson

8 Sing the Happy Birthday or Name Day song two or three times. Change Poppy's and Bean's names for the name of any pupil(s) in the class whose birthday is today or soon.

UNIT 5

Lesson One

Language focus
He's... She's... .

Revision: Greetings and introductions. Talking about age. The verb *to be*.

New words
Hi! hippopotamus

Revision/Warm-up

1 Start an Alphabet Chain. Pupils rapidly say one letter of the alphabet each in sequence. If they hesitate or are wrong, they are out.

Presentation (PUPIL'S BOOK p.17 CS13)

2 Play the first part of CS13 up to the 'pause' tone. Pupils listen and point to each of the speakers in turn. Kate and Ken introduce themselves on this page and are joined by Caroline and by Kevin, the hippo.

Tapescript

Voice 1: Listen and point.
   Kate: Hello, I'm Kate. I'm eight.
 Chorus: This is Kate. She's eight.
    Ken: Good morning, I'm Ken. I'm ten.
 Chorus: This is Ken. He's ten.
Caroline: Hi! I'm Caroline. I'm nine.
 Chorus: This is Caroline. She's nine.
  Kevin: I'm Kevin. I'm seven. I'm a hippopotamus.
 Chorus: This is Kevin. He's seven. He's a hippopotamus.

   [*pause tone]
Voice 1: Now listen and answer.
   Kate: Hello, I'm Kate. I'm eight.
          [pause for pupils to answer
          This is Kate. She's eight.]
    Ken: Good morning, I'm Ken. I'm ten.
          [pause for pupils to answer]
Caroline: Hi! I'm Caroline. I'm nine.
          [pause for pupils to answer]
  Kevin: I'm Kevin. I'm seven. I'm a hippopotamus.
          [pause for pupils to answer]

● Explain that *Hi* is an informal way to say *Hello*.
● Teach the contrasting meaning of *he* and *she* by pointing at boys and girls in the class and saying *This is George.* **He's** *nine... This is Mary.* **She's** *eight*, etc.

● Play the rest of CS13 now. Pupils listen to the characters introducing themselves and 'answer' by chanting back *This is... . He's/She's...*, reading from the page. Help pupils to imitate the rhythm and 'linking' they hear on the tape: *I'm eight... I'm a... . This is... He's a...* . Also help with pronunciation of *hippo'potamus.*

● Play the second 'Listen and answer' part of CS13 again to let pupils improve on their rhythm, linking and pronunciation.

Practice (PUPIL'S BOOK p.17)

3 Make a statement about any of the four characters on the page, at random: *He's seven ... She's nine.* Pupils listen and point to the character you are describing: *It's Kevin ... It's Caroline.*

● (Extra) Extend this simple listening game to refer to other characters in the book: *She's ten.* (Poppy); *He's nine.* (Woody); *He's a computer.* (Luke).

● Ask questions about each picture on p.17: *Who's this?* (Caroline) *How old is Caroline?* etc. Help pupils to use the right pronoun for the male and female characters.

4 Transfer: Ask pupils about each other: *Who's this? How old is...?* using the same questions as above. Help with the *he/she* distinctions if necessary.

Reading and writing (ACTIVITY BOOK p.17)

5 **Activity** ①Pupils read the speech bubbles and then complete the sentences below with *he* or *she*. Remind them to use capital letters at the beginning of sentences.

Answers	1. He	3. He	5. He
	2. She	4. She	6. She

6 **Activity** ②Pupils rewrite the sentences using *he* or *she*.

Answers	1. She's ten.	4. She's eight.
	2. He's ten.	5. He's ten.
	3. He's nine.	

Ending the lesson

7 Have one or two games of the Spelling Shark, using any known vocabulary. As far as possible, let pupils run the game themselves.

Lesson Two

Language focus
his and *her*

Revision: Numbers 0-10. Telephone numbers.

New words
bye café Come on! his her now OK river

Revision/Warm-up

1 Chant the Numbers Rhyme once or twice, with clapping, as before.

Story presentation

(PUPIL'S BOOK p.18, CS14)

2 *The River Café.* The story so far: Poppy and Bean have made a new friend, Woody. We have also been introduced briefly to the 'Captain' and her dog, Pluto. Now the story of the adventures of these characters together begins... .

● Before listening: Pre-teach some of the new words (leaving others to be explained after listening).Teach *river* and *café* by means of board sketches; teach *now* and *Come on* by mime and gesture. Drill the pronunciation of the words. Check that all pupils know the informal expression *OK*, used here as a question. Finally, remind pupils of the way phone numbers are given in English: *My telephone number is... What's your number?*

● Play CS14. Pupils listen and read.

● Play CS14 again. Pupils listen, read and repeat.

● After listening: Explain the meaning of *Meet me...* and ask pupils to guess what *Bye* must mean, since they already know *Goodbye.*

Story practice

3 Dialogue: Pupils in pairs read and practise **Picture 7 only**.

● One or two pairs act out the dialogue.

Presentation (PUPIL'S BOOK p.19)

4 *His bicycle... Her bicycle.* Read the sentences at the top of the page, pointing to the characters and their bicycles. Pupils listen and repeat.

● Transfer: Go round the class, talking about pupils and their possessions: *This is George. This is **his** pen. This is **his** bag... This is Mary. This is **her** ruler. This is **her** book,* etc.

Practice

5 Ask individual pupils to read out sentences 1 - 10 from page 19. The other pupils match the sentences with pictures a - j.
- Pupils write the letter for each picture in the box next to the right sentence.

Answers	1. d	3. c	5. h	7. e	9. f
	2. j	4. a	6. i	8. g	10. b

6 (Extra) Pair work: Pupils take turns to name any picture on p.19 by its letter, at random. Their partner responds by pointing to the picture of Ken or Kate and answering *It's his...* or *It's her...* , depending on who the object belongs to.

Writing (ACTIVITY BOOK p.18)

7 **Activity** ③ Pupils write the appropriate adjectives *his* or *her*.

Answers	1. her	3. his	5. her	7. his
	2. her	4. his	6. his	8. her

Ending the lesson

8 Play one or two games of Numbers Bingo! (see page 20).

Be prepared!

Bring the Feelie Bag to the next lesson. In the bag put small cards or squares of paper with one letter of the alphabet (a- z) on each.

Lesson Three

Language focus
Revision: The verb *to be.* All vocabulary.

Revision/Warm-up

1 Sing the Happy Birthday song for pupils whose birthday is today or soon.

2 (Extra)Game: The Feelie Bag should contain small cards or squares of paper, each with one of the small letters of the alphabet (a -z) on it.
- Divide pupils into two teams.
- Draw one letter-card out of the bag and challenge each team in turn to think of a word beginning with that letter. One team member then spells out the word suggested.
- Play several rounds for each team and keep scores on the board.

Practice (Revision) (PUPIL'S BOOK p.20)

3 *Bingo!* Pupils choose a 'block' of any **six pictures together** from anywhere on the page. Their pictures must be adjacent. They cover up all other pictures outside their 'block'.
- Play Bingo! by calling out words for any of the pictures on the page, at random. Pupils cover each of their chosen pictures that they hear you name. The first person to cover all six pictures in their 'block' calls out *Bingo!*
- Play two or three rounds. Pupils choose different 'blocks' of pictures each time.

4 (Extra) Pair work: Pupils take turns to name any picture on the page. Their partner listens and responds by pointing to the named picture and word. The aim is to go as fast as possible, playing 'word-tennis' backwards and forwards in this way until one of the pair makes a mistake. They can keep scores. Go round helping.

Reading and writing

(ACTIVITY BOOK pp.19 - 20)

5 AB p.19 **Activity** ④ Pupils complete the sentences by writing *am ('m)* or *is ('s)* in the gaps in the speech bubbles.
Answers
1. [Poppy] My name *is* Poppy. ... This *is* Bean.
2. [Woody] I'*m* nine. ... [Bean] I'*m* ten.

3. [Bean] And she's ten.

4. [Bean] Hello? This *is* 94312.

6 AB p.19 **Activity** ⑤ Pupils write sentences to describe the pictures.

Answers
1. It's an envelope. 2. It's an apple.
3. It's a doll. 4. It's a car.

7 AB p.20 **Activity** ⑥ Pupils complete the crossword with capital letters now they are familiar with the English alphabet. (English people usually use capital letters for crosswords.)

Answers

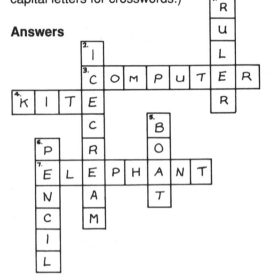

Ending the lesson

8 Finish with a Counting Chain round the class; sing the Alphabet Song or the Happy Birthday song; play any game pupils wish to repeat.

UNIT 6

Lesson One

Language focus
Asking for information (Yes/No questions): *Is it a/an...?*
Yes, it is./ No, it isn't.

New words
calculator

Revision/Warm-up

1 Play two or three games of Picture Bingo! (see Unit 5, Lesson 3; PB p.20) to revise vocabulary to be used later in this lesson. Ensure that the words *aeroplane*, *balloon* and *boat* are covered. Also revise the words *telephone* (mime and ask *What's this?*) and *hippopotamus* (point to Kevin on PB p.17, ask *Who's this?* and when pupils answer, say *Yes. He's a hippopotamus... a hippopotamus*.)

Presentation (PUPIL'S BOOK p.21)

2 *Is it an aeroplane?* Teach the new word *calculator* by a board sketch and with mime, or with the real object, if you have a pocket calculator.
Pupils listen and repeat.
● Question - Answer: Point to Picture 1 on the bottom half of p.21 and ask questions about it.
T: (pointing): *Is it an elephant?*
P: *No.*
T: *No, it isn't. Is it a hippo?*
P: *Yes.*
T: *Yes, it is. It's a hippo.*
● Point out the shortened form of the word *hippopotamus* here: *hippo*.
● Drill the short answers *Yes, it is* and *No, it isn't* several times, then ask about a different picture on the page, helping pupils to use the short answers correctly.
● Question - Answer: Point to one of the pictures and help pupils to ask you the question about it, using *Is it a/an...?* Answer their questions with short answers, as before. Ask and answer about only two or three of the pictures in this way to give a model for pupils' pair work in the next activity.

Practice (PUPIL'S BOOK p.21 CS15)

3 Pair work: Pupils look at the picture of Ken and Caroline at the top of p. 21. They listen as you read through the dialogue between the two characters, to demonstrate what they are doing here: they are asking each other questions about the puzzle picture.

● Pupils take turns to ask and answer about the picture puzzle on p. 21 in the same way, using the question *Is it a/an...?* and the short answers just presented. Go round helping.

4 CS15: Play CS15 right through once. Pupils listen.

● Play CS15 again, pausing after each short dialogue to let pupils point to the picture Caroline and Ken are looking at each time.

Answers   Picture 4 (a balloon)
Picture 6 (a boat)
Picture 5 (an aeroplane)
Picture 3 (a telephone)
Picture 1 (a hippo)

Tapescript

Ken: Is it a boat?
Caroline: Mmm. No. It isn't. Is it a balloon?
Ken: Yes, it is! *
Caroline: Look at this. Is it a boat?
Ken: Yes, it is.*
Ken: What's this? Is it an elephant?
Caroline: No, it isn't. It's an aeroplane.
Ken: Oh yes, it is.*

Caroline: Is this a calculator?
Ken: Mmm. No, it isn't. It's a telephone.*
Ken: And this is... an elephant.
Caroline: No, it isn't. It's a hippo.
Ken: Oh yes..., it's a hippo. *

[Note: Picture 2, the calculator, is not discussed on the tape.]

5 (Extra) Game: 'Guess'. Build up simple drawings, line by line on the board, as before (see page 21).

(a television)

(a boat)

(an aeroplane)

(a telephone)

After you add each new line pupils ask **you** questions:
P: *Is it a/an...?*   T: *Yes, it is* or *No, it isn't.*
If necessary, prompt pupils by asking
Is this a ...? Guess!

● Pair work: Pupils continue the drawing and guessing game, using any picture on PB p.20 as a model.

Reading and writing (ACTIVITY BOOK p.21)

6 Activity ①If necessary, revise the word *calculator* before pupils begin.

Answers   1. Yes, it is.   4. No, it isn't.
2. No, it isn't.   5. Yes, it is
3. Yes, it is.   6. Yes, it is.

7 Finish the lesson with one or two Numbers Races on the board or a Numbers Chain round the class.

Be prepared!

Bring the Feelie Bag to the next lesson. Also bring several pairs of known objects, one big and the other small (e.g. one big ball and the other very small; two different sized rulers, books, pencils, toy cars, bags, etc.)

Lesson Two

Language focus
The big/small (box) .

New words
box detective dog television big small

Revision/Warm-up

1 Use any of the simple board drawings, built up line by line as suggested previously in Unit 4, Lesson 2 or in Unit 6, Lesson 1. Pupils ask you: *Is it a/an...?* after each new line is added to the drawing, trying to guess what the picture is. Also introduce the alternative *Yes/No* question form *Is **this** a/an...?* here.

Story presentation

(PUPIL'S BOOK p.22, CS16)

2 *The detective.* The story so far: Poppy and Bean went to meet Woody at the River Café. He was knocked down by a runaway dog... .
   ● Before listening: Pre-teach the word *dog* with an example (*Pluto is a dog*) and do a mime or a sketch. Teach *detective* with examples of famous detectives pupils may know from television, or with a mime again. Drill the pronunciation of the new words.
   ● Play CS16. Pupils listen and read.
   ● Play CS16 again. Pupils listen and repeat.
   ● After listening: Ask questions about the characters in the story, all together here for the first time: use the *Yes/No* question *Is this Pluto? Is this Captain Shadow?*, etc. as shown in Picture 3 and help pupils to give the short answers.

Story practice

3 Dialogue: Pupils in pairs read and practise **Picture 3 only.**
   ● One or two pairs act out the dialogue.

Presentation (PUPIL'S BOOK p.23)

4 Books closed. The Feelie Bag. Put four or five **pairs** of objects into the bag - one big and the other small. Pupils name each object as it goes into the bag: *a ball... a book... a ruler...* etc.
   ● Feel one of the objects inside the bag. Make guesses:
   T: *What's this?... It's a ball.* etc.
   A pupil feels the bag too and then confirms or rejects the guess:

P: *Yes, it is./No, it isn't.*
   ● Pull the object out of the bag and name it, using *the* and either *big* or *small* to specify which of the pair of similar objects it is: *It's the **big** ball* or *It's the **small** ball*. Show the meaning of *big* and *small* by gesture. Pupils listen and repeat.
   ● Do this with all the objects one by one. Pupils listen and repeat each time.
   ● Put all the objects back into the bag. Take them out again one by one, as before, and ask *What's this?* each time, helping pupils to specify *It's the big ruler...* etc.
   ● Give the objects out to individual pupils round the room as each one is correctly specified.

[Note: If you don't have pairs of objects to use with the Feelie Bag use board drawings of big and small objects.]

Practice (PUPIL'S BOOK p.23, CS17)

5 (Extra) The 'Please and Thank you' game. Give specific instructions to individuals about the Feelie Bag objects now distributed round the class: *Show me the small ball*, etc. As in previous games, pupils should only react if you say *please*: T: *Show me the small ball.* - P: does not move. T: *Show me the small ball, please.* - P: points to the small ball.
   ● Play a few rounds and then let pupils take over as 'teacher'. If necessary, write up the 'cue' instruction *Show me...* on the board to help pupils.

6 *The small box and the big box.* Before listening: Pre-teach the new words *box* and *television* with simple sketches on the board.
   ● Pupils look at the pictures on PB p.23. Point to picture (a) and say *Here's the big box.* Then point to picture (e) and say *Here's the small box.* Point to picture (b) and say *Here's the small icecream.* Then ask pupils to *Point to the big icecream.* They point to picture (g).
   ● Continue in the same way.
   T: *Point to the big television.* (f)
      Point to the small television. (c)
      Point to the big elephant. (h)
      Point to the small elephant. (d)
   ● Play CS17. Pupils listen, look at the pictures, and point at the one they hear described on the tape.

Tapescript

Here's the big box.
Here's the small box.
It's the small icecream.

Look at the big television.
This is the small television.
Look! Here's the big elephant.

Answers   a... e... b... f... c... h

7 Pair work: Pupils take turns to point at random to any of the pictures on p.23 asking *What's this?* Their partner answers: *It's the big television... It's the small icecream...* etc. Go round helping.

8 *Language puzzle.* This will be the first time pupils have seen the words *television* and *small* in their written form: write them up on the board and practise reading them several times before beginning the puzzle.

Answers
1. It's the big television.   3.No, it isn't.
2. Is this the small icecream?   4. Yes,it is.

[Note: The question mark is the distinguishing feature for the difference between the correct endings for numbers 1 and 2.]

Reading (ACTIVITY BOOK p.22)

9 **Activity ②** Pupils match the sentences with the objects in the picture and write the identification letter of each object in the appropriate box.

Answers   1.c   3.d   5.e   7. f
               2.b   4.h   6.g   8.a

Ending the lesson

10 Play two games of the Spelling Shark with the new words *detective* and *television*.

Be prepared!

Bring the Feelie Bag and the small letter-cards (a-z), used in Unit 5, into the next lesson.

Lesson Three

Language focus
Links between letters and their sounds (phonics).

New words
happy   song

Revision/Warm-up

1 Use the picture on PB p.23. Say *Show me a...* . Pupils point to the named object.

Song presentation

(PUPIL'S BOOK p.24 CS18)

2 *The happy hippo.* Before listening: Pre-teach the new words *happy* by facial gesture and *song* by mime.
● Pay CS18. Pupils listen and follow in their books.
● Play CS18 again. Pupils listen again once or twice more and try to sing along with the tape.

3 *You say it!* Read out the tongue-twister at normal speed two or three times, going slightly faster each time.
● Get different pupils in turn to try saying the tongue-twister, also going as fast as they can without tripping over their words. Help them with the sentence rhythm:
Hello. Here's Henry the happy hippo'potamus!

Reading and writing

(ACTIVITY BOOK pp.23-24)

4 **Activity ③** (see Introduction,p.6 on phonics): This activity (and similar ones in following units) helps pupils to associate sounds of spoken English with the written letters. Pupils look at the first letter of a word and the sound it represents, e.g. *a* for *apple*.
● Say the words for each of the four pictures across the top: *a... apple, b... ball, c... car, d... dog.* Emphasize the sound at the beginning of each word. Pupils listen and read the four words.
● Demonstrate the activity by focusing only on *b* for *ball.* Write the word *ball* up on the board. Then point to the pictures in the middle of the page in turn and ask *What's this?* Repeat pupils' answers together with the word *ball* each time. If the word does not have the same sound at the beginning (e.g. *car... ball),* shake your head and say *No.* If it does have the same *b* sound at the beginning (e.g. *book... ball),* nod your head and say *Yes,* pointing to the

b of *ball*. Write the new word up underneath *ball* on the board. Collect all the *b* words in the exercise together in this way (*book, bicycle, balloon*).

● Finally say the word for each of the *b* pictures again in turn as you draw a line to link each of the pictures with the letter *b* at the top.

● If necessary, repeat the demonstration with the letter *c* to be sure that all pupils understand the linking task. Then ask them to draw lines in the same way to link each of the pictures with one of the four letters at the top, according to the sound of its first letter.

Answers	a - apple,
	b - book, bicycle, balloon,
	c - cassette, computer
	d - desk, doll

5 AB p.23 **Activity** ④ Pupils look at the pictures and write in the missing letters to complete the correct spelling of the four words.

Answers	1. telephone	3. detective
	2. dog	4. box

6 AB p.24 **Activity** ⑤ Pupils follow the tangled lines and write the words in the correct boxes.

Answers	ANIMALS - dog, elephant, hippo
	TOYS - balloon, doll, kite
	FOOD - orange, apple, icecream

Ending the lesson

7 Sing *The happy hippo* song again, using CS18 if necessary.

8 (Extra) Revise any known vocabulary from the previous pages of the PB or AB, using the Feelie Bag and the letter-cards as before in Unit 5 for a team spelling-challenge game. Teams take turns to think of any word beginning with the letter drawn out of the bag, and then challenge the other team to spell it.

UNIT 7

Lesson One

Language focus
Describing physical appearance.Possession: *I've got/ have got...* Adjectives of size: *long, short,* etc.

New words
ear eye face hair head mouth nose long short monster

Revision/Warm-up

1 Play the 'Please and Thank you' game. Give very specific instructions:
Show me the (small) ruler (please).
Show me the (big) pencil (please). etc.
Hand over to pupils. Help with the language, as necessary.

Presentation (PUPIL'S BOOK p.25)

2 Books closed. Pre-teach *face, eye, ear, mouth, nose* and *hair* by pointing at your own face and features (*This is my nose*, etc.). Also teach *long* and *short (hair)* by gesture.
● Pupils listen and repeat the new words.
● Speed drill the new words. Pupils point to parts of their face in response to instructions: *Show me your nose, please.* etc.

Practice (PUPIL'S BOOK p.25 CS19)

3 *I've got a big nose.* Pupils read through the labels on the picture Zoko is holding. They then look at the three pictures on the bottom half of the page as you pretend to be the man in Picture 1. Say *I am Number 1* and point to yourself and to the picture in turn. Then, if possible changing your voice a little for the act, say *I've got a big nose. I've got a big mouth. I've got small eyes. I've got small ears. I've got short hair.* Get pupils to point at each feature as you describe it. Show the contrast of *big* and *small* again by gesture.
● Pretend to be the man in Picture 3 in the same way, but this time as you give the description, pause and prompt pupils to supply the right adjective for each feature.

T: *I've got... big ears or small ears?*

P: *Big ears.*

T: *Yes. I've got big ears.*

Complete the description in this way (*big eyes, a big mouth, a small nose, long hair*).

4 Explain that one of the three men is Mr X, the robber. Mr X will describe himself on the tape. Play CS19 once through. Pupils listen and look at the three 'photos' on the bottom of p. 25.

Tapescript

Mr X: Listen, friend...
This is my face.
I've got small eyes.
I've got big ears.
I've got a small mouth.
I've got a big nose,
and I've got long hair. OK, friend?
I'm Mr X,..... OK?

● Play CS19 again. Pupils listen and try to identify which of the three 'photos' is Mr X.
● Play CS19 again, if necessary. Pupils listen and check.

Answer   No. 2 is Mr X.

5 PB p.25. Give a full, short description of either of the other two 'photos' in a similar way. Pupils listen and match, as before.

● (Extra) Pair work: Pupils take turns to choose any one of the three 'photos' and pretend to be that character, giving a description of 'my' face, as on the tape. Their partner listens, as above, and tries to identify which photo it is. Go round helping with the new language.

● Finally, point out the short form - long form linking of *I've got* and *have got* on the board, showing which letters the apostrophe replaces in the shortened form: *I have got* → *I've got.*

Reading and writing (ACTIVITY BOOK p.25)

6 **Activity** ①Pre-teach *head* (pointing at your own), and *monster* (showing the picture).
● Write the new words and the adjectives *long* and *short* up on the board and drill their pronunciation as pupils read them out together and then individually.
● Pupils look at the picture of the monster on AB p.25 and individuals in turn suggest adjectives to fill the gaps in the speech bubble. Then all pupils write the missing words into the speech bubble, as in the example.

Answers   big head...   two big eyes...
two small eyes...   big nose...
short hair...   small ears...   big mouth

Ending the lesson

7 Finish with *The happy hippo* song, using CS18, if necessary.

Be prepared!

Ask pupils to bring in photos of members of their family and of various friends.
Bring in similar photos of your family too.

Lesson Two

Language focus
Members of the family: *This is my father*, etc.
Possession: *He's got.../ She's got....*

New words

brother	family	Dad/father	friend
Mum/mother	robber	sister	letter

Revision/Warm-up

1 Memory game. Pupils close their books and try to name as many of the 24 pictures on PB p.20 as they can from memory. Record the words on the board.

Story presentation

(PUPIL'S BOOK p.26, CS20)

2 *Mr X is in London.* The story so far: The three children have met the famous detective, Captain Shadow. Now Captain Shadow gets in touch with them again... .
● Books closed. Before listening: Pre-teach the meaning of *letter* (show one), *friend* (give examples of pairs of friends in the class) and *robber* (copy the picture on p.31 of the AB). The word *telephone* is being used as a verb for the first time, but its meaning should be easy to understand.
● Play CS20. Pupils listen and read.
● Play CS20 again. Pupils listen and repeat after each speaker.
● After listening: Point out the short form - long form linking of *We've got* and *We have got,* showing on the board which letters are replaced by the apostrophe in the shortened form:
We have got... → *We've got...*
Also check that pupils know where London is!

Story practice

3 Dialogue: Pupils in pairs read and practise **Pictures 5 and 6 only.** Go round helping.
   ● One or two pairs act out the dialogue.

Presentation (PUPIL'S BOOK p.27)

4 Show pupils your own photographs of members of your family. Say *This is my family - here's my (mother)... I've got (two brothers)* etc.
   ● Ask about pupils' photographs (which they should have brought in): *Is this your (brother)?* etc.
   ● Pupils repeat *This is my mother... This is my friend* etc. after you.
   ● Explain that in English *mother* is often called *Mum* and *father* is often called *Dad.*
   ● Drill pronunciation of the new family words.

> ● (Extra) Pair work: Pupils exchange personal photographs and ask each other in turn: *Who's this? Is this your (father)?* etc.

Reading

(PUPIL'S BOOK p.27, ACTIVITY BOOK p.26)

5 *This is my family.* Read through Lucy's introduction of her family. Pupils listen and read.
   ● Point out the short form - long form linking of *She's got* and *She has got,* showing on the board which letters are replaced by the apostrophe in the shortened form: *He has got... → He's got... She has got... → She's got...*
   ● Ask pupils to take turns to read one sentence each from Lucy's speech bubbles out loud. Help with pronunciation as necessary.

> ● (Extra) Pretend to be Lucy. Make simple statements about her family, some right and some wrong: *My mother has got big eyes... My father has got a happy face... My sister, Annie, has got short hair... My friend, Nick, has got a big mouth... My brother, Herman, is ten... My brother, Shep, has got short hair* etc.
> Pupils listen and look at the picture. They decide if your statements are true or not and answer *Yes* or *No* to them accordingly.

6 AB p.26 **Activity ②** Pre-teach the word *little* (by gesture) as it is used to refer to younger, and usually also smaller, brothers and sisters.
   ● Pupils look at the 'photo' of the family, read the sentences, and decide if they are right or wrong. They circle the tick or cross accordingly.

Answers   1.✓   3.x   5.✓
           2.x   4.✓

Writing (ACTIVITY BOOK p.26)

7 Activity ③ Pupils draw their own face in the frame on the left. They then complete the three sentences with *big, small, long* or *short,* as appropriate to themselves and write in the labels for the parts of the face.

Ending the lesson

8 Play one or two games of the Spelling Shark, using any of the new family words.

Lesson Three

Language focus
The verb *to be* cont: *You are   You're*

New words
boy   girl   Right!

Revision/Warm-up

1 Revise vocabulary for the face and hair, asking *What's this?* and *Is your (hair) long or short?* etc.

Presentation (PUPIL'S BOOK p.28, CS21)

2 *A game: Who am I?* Pre-teach *girl* and *boy.* Point at individual girls and boys and say *(Mary) is a girl. (George) is a boy.* Pupils repeat after you.
   ● Ask questions about the four pictures across the top of PB p.28: *Is Annie a boy or a girl?... How old is she?... Is Herman a boy or a girl?... How old is he?*
   ● Play CS21: This is an example of the 'Who am I?' guessing game. Pupils listen and read.
   ● After listening: Show the short form - long form linking of *You are* and *You're* in the usual way on the board. Also point out the word *Right!* and the short answers to the *Are you...?* question: *Yes, I am. / No, I'm not.*

Practice

3 Play the 'Who am I?' game. Give one pupil the 'false identity' of one of the four characters at the top of the page, on a strip of paper: *You are (Lucy/ Shep* etc.)
   ● The other pupils ask questions, as in the PB p.28 cartoon strip, to find out who the pupil is pretending to be. Play several rounds with the different

identities. Encourage pupils to use the adjectives they know (*Is your hair long or short?* etc.).
● Include other monster characters in the game, using the picture on PB p.27.

Reading (ACTIVITY BOOK pp.27-8)

4 Activity ④ This is the second activity to help pupils associate spoken sounds with written letters.
● Say the words for each of the four pictures across the top: *e... elephant, f... football, g... girl, h... hippo.* Emphasize the sound at the beginning of each word. Pupils listen and read the four words.
● Demonstrate the activity in the same way as recommended in Unit 6, Lesson 3. Focus on only one of the four model words, writing it up on the board, as before. Then point to the pictures in the middle of the page in turn and help pupils to link together the words with the same sound at the beginning, writing the new words underneath the model word already on the board.
● Finally, say the word for each of the group of pictures with the same initial sound again in turn as you draw a line to link each picture with the appropriate letter at the top.
● If necessary, repeat the demonstration with another letter in the same way, to be sure that all pupils understand the linking task. Then ask them to draw lines to link each of the pictures with one of the four letters at the top, according to the sound of its first letter.

Answers   e - elephant, envelope
              f - family
              g - girl
              h - hair, hippo

5 AB p.27 **Activity ⑤** Pupils read the words in the box and circle only the family words.

Answers   mother   sister
              father   brother

6 AB p.28 **Activity ⑥** Pupils match the sentences with the characters and write the identification letter of the character in the box.

Answers   1.a   2.d   3.b   4.e   5.f   6.c

Ending the lesson

7 Sing *The happy hippo* song or play a game or two of 'Who's this?', using the blindfold, as pupils wish.

UNIT 8

Lesson One

Language focus
Asking about possession: *Have you got...? Yes, I have / No, I haven't. Has she/he got...? Yes, she/he has. No, she/he hasn't.*

New words
cousin comic (Are you) ready?

Revision/Warm-up

1 Play a few rounds of the Spelling Shark to revise the vocabulary needed for this lesson: *orange, umbrella, cassette.*

Presentation (PUPIL'S BOOK p.29, CS22)

2 *Have you got your bag?* Context: the two little monster sisters, Lucy and Annie, are going to the beach. They are taking two bags, shown on the right.
● Books closed. Before listening: Pre-teach *Are you ready?* This can become a useful piece of regular classroom English from now on. Just before playing CS22, ask *Are you ready?* Also pre-teach *comic*, either by showing one or by pointing to the comic in bag B, 'The Bucket'.
● Ask pupils *What is in the two bags?* They look and answer: *an umbrella, a doll, a book, a comic*, etc. Explain that, in the recording, Lucy is checking with Annie that they have everything they need.
● Play CS22. Pupils listen and point to Annie's bag.

Tapescript

Lucy: Are you ready, Annie?
Annie: Yes. I'm ready.
Lucy: Have you got your book?
Annie: Yes, I have.
Lucy: Have you got your pencil?
Annie: No, I haven't. It's in your bag.
Lucy: Have you got your two cassettes?
Annie: Yes, I have.
Lucy: Have you got the apples?
Annie: Yes. I have. And you've got the oranges. OK?
Lucy: OK. Come on!

Answer Annie's bag is bag A.

● After listening: Teach *Have you got...? Yes, I have./ No, I haven't.* Read through the speech bubbles of Annie and Lucy.

Practice

3 Write up the *Have you got...?* question and the short *Yes/No* answers. Ask questions to practise the patterns:

T: *Have you got a pen, Mary?*
P: *Yes, I have.*
T: *Have you got a comic in your bag, George?*
P: *No, I haven't.*etc.

● Pair work: Pupils ask each other similar questions. Go round helping them to use the short answers correctly.

4 Transfer: Ask pupils more questions about them-selves now: *Have you got a kite/bicycle/boat?* etc.

Presentation

5   Introduce the Third Person form of the question and answers (*Has he/she got...? Yes, (s)he has./No, (s)he hasn't*). by asking questions about Lucy and Annie and their bags:

T: *Look at Lucy's bag. Has she got her umbrella?*
P: *Yes.*
T: *Yes, she has.*
T: *Has she got her ruler?*
P: *No.*
T: *No, she hasn't.*

● Drill the questions and short answers. Point out the written forms which are given in the dialogue between Zoko and Kate, at the bottom.

Practice

6 Pair work: One pupil asks his or her partner about Lucy's bag (bag B): *Has she got a comic? Has she got an envelope?* etc. The other pupil asks his or her partner about Annie's bag (bag A) in the same way.

7 (Extra) Game. Pupils close their books. Write up the following check list on the board. Do not write in the ticks and crosses.

	A: Annie	B: Lucy
a boat	x	✓
a pen	✓	x
an envelope	✓	x
a ruler	x	✓
an umbrella	✓	x
an apple	✓	x
a book	✓	✓
a doll	✓	x
a cassette	✓	✓
a ball	x	✓

● Ask first about bag A, then about bag B: *Has Annie got a boat in her bag? Has Lucy got a boat in her bag?* Pupils try to answer from memory only. Fill in the ticks and crosses against each item on the list on the board now, according to what the pupils agree. The correct answers are on the diagram. At the end pupils open their books again and see how well they remembered.

● Pupils then ask **you** questions, with your own book closed.

Reading and writing (ACTIVITY BOOK p.29)

8 **Activity** ①Pupils read the *Have you got...?* questions and write true answers.

9 **Activity** ②Pre-teach the word *cousin* - use a simple family tree sketch on the board to explain this. Then ask individuals *Have you got a cousin? What's his/her name? How old is your cousin?*

● Pupils read Lucy's speech bubble. They match the description with one of the three 'photos' below.

Answers   Daisy is Picture C.
1. Yes, she has.
2. Yes, she has.
3. No, she hasn't.

Ending the lesson

10 Finish with rhymes or with a song.

Lesson Two

Language focus
Describing people.

New words
aunt (auntie) uncle man woman boss fat thin happy sad old young tall short

Revision/Warm-up

1 Revise *Have you got...?* questions by asking pupils what they have got in their bags.
T: *Have you got a pen/a cassette/a comic/a book, etc. in your bag?*
P: *Yes, I have./ No, I haven't.*

Story presentation

(PUPIL'S BOOK p.30, CS23)

2 *They've got Captain Shadow.* The story so far: Poppy and Bean received a message from Captain Shadow, asking them to phone her computer, Luke. Luke told them to go to the river to meet Captain Shadow there.
● Before listening: Pre-teach *woman, man* (*Captain Shadow is a woman, Mr X is a man*) and *boss*. Drill pronunciation of the new words.
● Play CS23. Pupils listen and read.
● Play CS23 again. Pupils listen, read and repeat.
● After listening: Ensure that the meaning of *they* (= *he* and *she*) is quite clear to pupils, and also point out the short form *they've...* and explain its linking to the long form *they have.*
● Go through all the different forms of *have got* now, listing them on the board for pupils to copy and memorize: *I've got...*
  You've got...etc.
A complete table of the verb form is given on PB p.59.

Story practice

3 Ask a few simple questions about the story: *Who is the man? Who is the woman? Has Mr X got a boat? Has Lifter got an envelope in Picture 2? Has she got her envelope in Picture 5? Have Mr X and Lifter got Captain Shadow in the boat?*

4 Dialogue:Pupils in pairs practise and then act out the dialogue of **Picture 5 only.**

Presentation (PUPIL'S BOOK p.31)

5 PB p.31 *Old and young, fat and thin.* Teach the contrasted adjectives in the top half of the page by means of gesture and examples: *You are young, my mother is old... George is tall, Mary is short,* etc.
● Ask individual pupils to read out any of the set of eight adjectives at random. The others listen and mime the meaning of the word. Read and mime all the words in this way.

Song presentation (PUPIL'S BOOK p.31)

6 *The family song.* Before listening: Pre-teach *uncle* and *aunt*, using the same sketched family tree diagram as suggested in the previous lesson. Revise *cousin* in this way also:

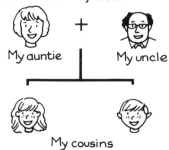

● Teach and practise the song as usual.
● Play CS24 again two or three times. Encourage pupils to sing along.
● After listening: Get pupils to guess and mime the meaning of the word *lazy*, using the picture of Cousin Daisy to help them. With less shy pupils ask: *Are you lazy, George?* etc. Also ask pupils about their 'extended' families: *Have you got an auntie/a cousin?* etc.

Practice

7 (Extra) Game: Word pairs. Write up adjectives at random on the board: *fat, big, young, long, short, small, thin, old.* Pupils match them into pairs (*fat + thin*).

Reading and writing (ACTIVITY BOOK p.30)

8 Activity ③ Pupils find the right answer to each question by following the tangled line from the character on the left to one of the dogs on the right. They then write in the answer.

Answers
1. No, he hasn't.	5. Yes, she has.
2. Yes, he has.	6. Yes, she has.
3. Yes, she has.	7. No, she hasn't.
4. No, she hasn't.	8. Yes, she has.

Ending the lesson

9 Sing *The family song* again, using CS24, if necessary.

Lesson Three

Language focus

Article + adjective + noun: *a + big + nose.*

Revision/Warm-up

1 Play a game of anagrams on the board, using the new words learnt in this unit.
Write up these words with their letters in jumbled order:
SCOUNI (cousin), PYPHA (happy), ZYLA (lazy), GUYON (young), HINT (thin), LALT (tall), CELUN (uncle), ADS (sad), MOCCI (comic).
Pupils work out and write the correctly spelled words.

Reading (PUPIL'S BOOK p.32)

2 *Two faces.* Pupils read the two short sections of the text either silently to themselves for a minute or two, or they read aloud in turn, sentence by sentence, round the class. Help their understanding of the passage with gestures and by pointing at parts of your own face.
[Note: If they read the texts aloud, also help them with the rhythm and linking of the language, to improve their overall fluency: e.g. This͜ is..., big͜ eyes..., He's͜ got͜ a... .]

● In answering the questions there are three options: **a.** Pupils can try to read and answer the questions at the bottom of the page on their own, silently writing down their answers. **b.** They can work together in pairs to find and agree on the right answers. **c.** The answers can be found all together as a class before pupils write them down. Choose which method will best suit your particular class.

Answers   1. Yes, he has.   4. No, she hasn't.
              2. No, she hasn't.   5. Yes, she has.
              3. No, he hasn't.   6. Yes, he has.

Reading and writing

(ACTIVITY BOOK pp.31-2)

3 **Activity** ④ Pupils say the words for each of the five pictures across the top: *i... icecream, k... kite, l...letter, m... man, n... nose.* They listen especially to the sound of the initial letters of the five words.
● They then say the word for each of the pictures below and match its initial sound with its initial letter at the top, drawing a line to link the picture and the letter, as before, (see Units 6 and 7, Lesson 3).

Answers   i - icecream   m - man, mouth, monster
              k - kite   n - nose
              l - letter

4 AB p.31 **Activity** ⑤ Pupils choose one of the seven adjectives from the box to complete each of the sentences.

Answers   1. tall   3. old   5. sad   7. thin
              2. short   4. happy   6. fat

5 AB p.32 **Activity** ⑥ Pupils find and circle the words hidden in the letter square.

Answers

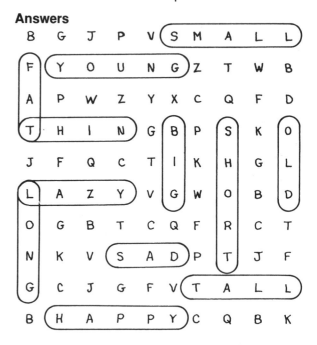

Ending the lesson

6 Play any game, sing a song or chant a rhyme, as pupils wish.

7 (Extra) Pupils make their own masks at home, like those on PB p.32, using paper plates, coloured crayons, wool etc.
● They write an information box about their mask, using the following framework (copied from the board):
This is . . . .
(S)he's got . . . . eyes.
(S)he's got a . . . . nose.
(S)he's got a . . . . mouth.
(S)he's got . . . . hair.
● Pupils can copy pictures of real (African, Japanese, Indian) masks from books and give the appropriate details if they wish. These could form the basis of a colourful classroom wall display.

UNIT 9

Lesson One

Language focus

Ability: *can* and *can't*. *Can you see the...?*
Yes, I can./ No, I can't.

New words

banana	monkey	bird	see
cage	zoo	hear	lion

Revision/Warm-up

1 Write anagrams on the board - *pipoh* and *helpneat* - and explain to pupils that they are the names of two animals (*hippo* and *elephant*).

Presentation (PUPIL'S BOOK p.33)

2 *Can you see an elephant?* Books closed. Pre-teach the words *bird, lion, monkey* and *snake* by simple board drawings with supporting mime. Copy the pictures on AB p.61 if necessary. Also teach the word *banana* now. Write the new words up and drill their pronunciation from the written words.
● Question - Answer: Pupils look at the picture puzzle at the top of PB p.33. Mime looking for something in the picture, as if it was very difficult to see. Ask pupils: *Can you see a lion?* Get one pupil to answer *Yes*, then expand the answer to *Yes, I can.*
● Drill the answer form. Ask more questions: *Can you see a hippo? Can you see a monkey? Can you see a big box?* etc. Pupils answer each time: *Yes, I can.*
● To teach *No, I can't* ask questions about things that are not in the picture: *Can you see an umbrella? Can you see a ball? Can you see a boy?* etc. Pupils answer *No.* Expand this answer to *No, I can't* and drill the new form.

Answers

These things are in the picture: a snake, two elephants, a monkey, a lion, a hippo, four birds, oranges, apples, bananas, a river, a box.

Practice

3 Pair work: Pupils take turns to ask each other *Can you see...?* questions about the things they can or cannot see in the PB p.33 picture puzzle. Go round helping with the new words and the question and answer forms.

Song presentation

(PUPIL'S BOOK p.33, CS25)

4 *The zoo song.* Pre-teach the new words *zoo* (name a local zoo) and *cage* (draw a board sketch). Also teach the word *hear.* Turn the volume of the cassette very low as you start the tape and ask *Can you hear the song?* Drill the new words.
● Play CS25. Present and practise the new song in the usual way, encouraging pupils to sing along once or twice with the tape as soon as they can.

Reading and writing (ACTIVITY BOOK p.33)

5 Activity ①Pupils read the questions and look at the picture above to find the right answers. They write in *Yes, I can.* or *No, I can't.* as appropriate.

Answers	1. Yes, I can.	5. No, I can't.
	2. Yes, I can.	6. Yes, I can.
	3. No, I can't.	7. Yes, I can.
	4. Yes, I can.	8. No, I can't.

Ending the lesson

6 Finish with a round or two of the Spelling Shark, using any of the new animal words which may still be written up on the board as cues.

Be prepared!

Bring a large handkerchief or scarf to the next lesson, for a blindfold.

Lesson Two

Language focus
Possession: *Whose...? Possessive__'s.*
Specifying location : *in.*

New words
bank catch city giraffe map perhaps photograph plan problem Quick! read

Revision/Warm-up

1 Get different pupils in turn to try to say the tongue-twister from PB p.24 again as fast as they can: *Hello. Here's Henry the happy hippopotamus.*

Story presentation

(PUPIL'S BOOK p.34, CS26)

2 *Mr X's plan.* The story so far: The three children have gone to meet Captain Shadow at the river in the evening, but they find that she has been captured by Mr X the robber and his friend, Lifter. They see Captain Shadow tied up in the cabin of Mr X's big boat.
● Before listening: Pre-teach some of the key words for this new story episode: *photograph, map, bank, plan* and *catch.* Teach these by showing real objects, by naming examples of local banks, and by mime (*catch*). Leave the other new words to discuss after the pupils have heard the story.
● Play CS26. Pupils listen and read.
● Play CS26 again. Pupils listen and repeat after each speaker.
● After listening: Ask pupils to try to guess the meaning of the words *Quick! read* and *perhaps* from the pictures, from their context in the story, and from the tone of the speakers. If necessary, play CS26 again to help them make guesses.

Story practice

3 Ask a few simple questions in English about the p. 34 story, pointing at the pictures: *In Picture 1, can Mr X see the twins? In Picture 3, what has Woody got? Has Poppy got the photo of Lifter in Picture 4? In Picture 6, can Captain Shadow read the name of the bank? What is the name of the bank?* etc.
4 Dialogue: Pupils read and practise **Pictures 5 and 6 only.** Go round helping.
● One or two pairs act out the dialogue.

Presentation (PUPIL'S BOOK p.35, CS27)

5 *Whose cage is this?* Context: the zoo-keeper has come to work in the morning and she has found that all the naughty animals have changed their cages, and the monkey has pulled all the labels off the cages as well. The zoo-keeper telephones her boss to tell him about the problem.
● Before listening: Pre-teach the words *problem* and the only unknown animal: *giraffe.* The word *in* (a place) can be left for passive recognition and understanding, unless it causes problems for pupils.
● Play CS27. Pupils listen and look at the pictures.

Tapescript

Keeper: Hello, boss! We've got a bad problem here.
Boss: What's the problem?
Keeper: All the animals are in the wrong cages.
The lion is in the bird's cage .....
The bird is in the monkey's cage ....
The monkey is in the snake's cage ....
The snake is in the hippo's cage ....
The hippo is in the giraffe's cage ....
The giraffe is in the lion's cage ....
And I don't know what to do ....

● Play CS27 again. Stop after the first statement. (*The lion is in the bird's cage.*) Point to Picture (B) with the lion and say *Here's the lion. Is this the lion's cage?* Pupils answer *No. It's the bird's cage* and then write *bird's cage* on the label at the bottom of that cage.
● Pause the tape after each statement to give pupils time to find and point to the animal mentioned. Check that they have all found the right animal, and then ask *Whose cage is this?* Play the tape again, if necessary, to let pupils listen again. They then write the name of the real owner of the cage in the blank label.

Answers
A the monkey's cage
B the bird's cage
C the hippo's cage
D the giraffe's cage
E the lion's cage
F the snake's cage

● After listening: Point out the form and meaning of the possessive singular__'s now, giving several examples of pupils' own possessions in the classroom: *This is Mary's desk. ... This is George's desk,* etc. Write up several examples on the board and show how the apostrophe__'s is added to the end of proper names or nouns to indicate ownership i.e. ... *the desk of Mary/George.*

Practice

6 Drill *Whose...?*, the possessive singular__ *'s* and the new words several times.
T: *Look at the monkey. Whose cage is he in? Is it the bird's cage or the snake's cage?*
P: *The snake's cage.*
T: *Yes, the monkey is in the snake's cage.* etc.

> ● (Extra) Pair work: Pupils take turns to ask and answer in the same way, using PB p.35 pictures again:
> P1: *Who is in the bird's cage?*
> P2: *The lion is in the bird's cage.* etc.

7 Transfer: Collect one possession from each pupil. Name each one in turn: *Anna's rubber*, etc. Put all the objects in a pile on the table.
● Teach the question *Whose...?* again: *Whose (pen) is this?* Drill the question several times:
T: *Whose pen is this?*
P: *It's Mary's pen*, etc.
● Pupils come out in turn and make guesses about objects (*This is Anna's ruler*) or ask questions (*Whose ruler is this? Is this George's ruler?*).

> ● (Extra) Game. Choose a pupil to be blind - folded. Other pupils place one object from the table in the blindfolded person's hands and make a true or false statement about it: *This is Susan's ruler. This is John's bag*, etc. The blindfolded pupil decides if the statement is right or wrong. If wrong, then the true owner or object must be named: *No, it isn't. It's Mary's ruler*, etc.

Reading and writing (ACTIVITY BOOK p.34)

8 Activity ② Pupils follow the tangled kite strings down from each of the animal kites to the children to find whose kite it is. They then write in the appropriate owner's name in the spaces in the sentences.

Answers	1. Annie's	4. Ken's
	2. Lucy's	5. Caroline's kite
	3. Shep's	6. Herman's kite

Ending the lesson

9 Sing *The zoo song*, using CS25 if necessary.

Be prepared!

Bring in the handkerchief or scarf again as a blindfold.

Lesson Three

Language focus
Giving/following directions.

New words
Turn right/left. Go straight on.

Revision/Warm-up

1 Pick up pupils' possessions at random. Ask other pupils *Is this Mary's bag or George's bag?* etc.

Presentation (PUPIL'S BOOK p.36)

2 Books closed. Teach the meaning of *Turn right, Turn left,* and *Go straight on* by hand gestures and by moving round the room. Drill the new words.
● Choose one or two pupils in turn to move round the room as you give instructions: *Turn right!... Stop!* etc. Pupils repeat each instruction after you.

3 *Turn left, turn right.* Pupils open their books and read the four instructions at the top.

Practice (PUPIL'S BOOK p.36, CS28)

4 *Can you find the cage?* Context: Pupils are at the zoo with Zoko. They must listen to the instructions on how to get to the different animals' cages.
● Play CS28. Pupils listen and trace with their fingers the route they are instructed to follow to the bird's cage. It will help them to follow more easily if they turn the book round each time they have turned and are therefore always pointing straight ahead after each turn.
[Note: When moving straight forwards they should automatically *Stop* whenever they come to any possible turning and wait to be told by the tape whether or not to turn there.]

Tapescript

Zoko: The bird's cage, please.
Kate: Turn left... Go straight on... Stop!... Turn right...go straight on ... and go straight on.
Zoko: The hippo's cage, please.
Kate: Turn right... Go straight on... Stop!... Turn left... Go straight on... Turn left.

● Play CS28 again to let pupils repeat and practise.

5 Pair work: Pupils take turns to ask each other for directions to any one of the cages in the zoo-maze. Again, they should automatically *Stop* whenever they have just made a turn and wait for the next instruction from their partner (e.g. *Go straight on*); they should also stop whenever they come to a possible turning and wait to be told whether or not to turn there, as before.

Reading and writing

(ACTIVITY BOOK pp.35-6)

6   **Activity ③** Pupils say the words for each of the four pictures across the top: **o... orange, p...pen, r...robber, s... snake.** They listen especially to the sound of the initial letters of the four words.
    ● They then say the word for each of the pictures below and match its initial sound with its initial letter at the top, drawing a line to link the picture and the letter.

Answers	o-orange	r-rubber, ruler, river
	p-pen, pencil	s-snake

7   AB p.35 **Activity ④** Pupils write in the missing letters to complete the words.

Answers	1. monkey	2. snake
	3. bird	4. elephant

8   AB p.36 **Activity ⑤** Pupils read the questions on the left and match them with the answers on the right.

Answers	1.d	2.b	3.a	4.c

9   AB p.36 **Activity ⑥** Pupils try out the puzzles on each other, attempting to say the alphabet in reverse order and read the message, and then trying to work out how to draw the picture puzzle of the triangle.

Ending the lesson

10   (Extra) Game. 'What can I see?' Look for a known object, easily visible, e.g. a rubber. Don't name it or look at it.
Say *One, two, three. What can I see? I can see something beginning with...* **R.**
● Drill this little chant a few times, so that the pupils can use it to play the game themselves.
● Pupils look for objects beginning with **R** and make guesses. When they guess correctly, they have to spell out the whole word:
R... U... B... B... E... R.
● Play several rounds, letting pupils take over as soon as possible.

Be prepared!

Bring the blindfold to the next lesson also.

UNIT 10

Lesson One

Language focus
Adjectives of colour: *the blue bicycle... the red bicycle.*
Revision: *have got.*

New words
black   blue   green   red   white   yellow   colour

Revision/Warm-up

1   Play a directions game using the maze on PB p.36 again.

Presentation (PUPIL'S BOOK p.37)

2   *Colours.* Say the names of the six colours across the top of the page one by one, pointing to the colour flash in the book. Pupils point to that colour flash on the page and read/repeat the colour word after you.
    ● Drill the pronunciation of each colour adjective two or three times. Also teach and drill the word *colour(s).*

Practice (PUPIL'S BOOK p.37, CS29)

3   *A game: Show me the green kite.* Remind pupils that they should point at the objects named.
    ● Play CS29. Pupils listen, and point to the object named on the tape.

Tapescript

The green kite... the blue doll... the red bicycle...
the black television... the white icecream...
the black telephone... the white television...
the yellow doll... the blue bicycle...
the green icecream... the red telephone...
the yellow kite.

● Play CS29 again. Pupils try to improve on their first attempt.
● Pair work: One pupil says *Show me... the green icecream.* Their partner points to the object named. Go round helping with vocabulary and pronunciation.

4   (Extra) Speed drill the new colour adjectives, using objects in the classroom:
T: *Show me...... a blue bag. ... a green book. ... a red pen,* etc.

Ask *Whose bag/book is it?* to revise *Whose?*
● Let pupils take over as teacher as soon as possible.

5 Transfer: Ask questions about objects in the classroom: *What colour is this* (*book*)*?* etc. Help pupils to remember and use the correct colour adjective each time.
● Also ask pupils about their own and each other's possessions:
What colour is Mary's (*pen*)*?*
... is your bag?
... is your family's car?
... is your bicycle? etc.
● Let pupils take over as 'teacher' and ask you questions.

Reading and writing (ACTIVITY BOOK p.37)

6 **Activity** ①Ask questions about the pictures, e.g.
Has the bird got an orange? Has the dog got a ball?
Is the lion on a bicycle? Is the lion in a box? etc.
● Pupils then complete the sentences by writing in the correct animal's name from the box at the top.

Answers 1. bird 2. monkey 3. dog 4. snake
5. lion 6. elephant

● Pupils read the completed sentences and colour in the objects with the colour specified in each sentence.

Ending the lesson

7 Play a few games of *'What can I see?'* (see Unit 9, Lesson 3). After each object has been guessed correctly, ask pupils *What colour is ...?* Let pupils take over.

Lesson Two

Language focus
Vocabulary for clothing. Making a suggestion: *Let's... .*

New words
blouse   coat   jeans   shirt   shoes   socks   trousers
a pair of....   brown   pink   newspaper   watch (verb)

Revision/Warm-up

1 Play a few rounds of the Spelling Shark with the new colour adjectives.

Story presentation

(PUPIL'S BOOK p.38, CS30)

2 *The big white boat.* The story so far: The three children rescued Captain Shadow from Mr X's boat. As they were escaping, Woody found the envelope which had been dropped by Lifter - her photo was in it, and there was a map with The Big City Bank written on it too. Captain Shadow guessed that Mr X had a plan about the bank... . [Ask pupils why Mr X wants to go to a bank. (To rob it.)]
● Before listening: Pre-teach *newspaper* (show one) and the verb *watch* (by mime).
● Play CS30. Pupils listen and read.
● Play CS30 again. Pupils listen and repeat.
● After listening: Point out that the question *See?* is a short form of *Can you see?* Also point out the use of *Let's...* to make suggestions, as Poppy does in Picture 5. This can be used as regular classroom language from now on: *Let's sing... Let's play... again.* etc.

Story practice

3 Ask a few questions in English about the PB p.38 story, pointing at the pictures: *Whose picture is in the newspaper? Whose big boat is this? What colour is Mr X's boat?* etc.
4 Dialogue: Pupils in pairs read and practise **Pictures 6 and 7 only** (Poppy and Woody).
● One or two pairs act out the dialogue.

Presentation (PUPIL'S BOOK p.39, CS31)

5 *The clothes rhyme.* Play CS31. Pupils listen and follow the rhyme in their books.
● Play CS31 again. Pupils listen and repeat several times.
● Pupils chant the rhyme without the tape, first together and then individually, if they wish.

● Teach the words for clothes one by one, pointing to your own clothes or to those of pupils in the class. Drill the pronunciation of the new words. Point out that *shoes, socks, jeans* and *trousers* are all plural because they are usually *a pair of...* (two together).

Practice

6 Ask questions about the colours of the clothes on the washing line, using *a pair of...* for the socks, trousers, jeans and shoes so that the answer is always *It's* (*red/blue* etc.) e.g. *What colour is the shirt? What colour is the skirt? What colour is the pair of shoes?*
 ● Teach the two new colours *brown* (*coat*) and *pink* (*blouse*) now by pointing to them. Drill these two new colour words and then ask questions to help pupils to use them: *What colour is the blouse? ... is Mary's skirt?* etc.

7 *Language puzzle: Who is it?* Pupils read the items on the list of clothes and match it with one of the four characters in the picture. Who has got those clothes?

Answer   Annie.

(Extra) Pair work: Pupils play a game of 'Who is it?', taking turns to pretend to be one of the four characters in PB p.39.
e.g. (Pupil 2 is pretending to be Lucy):
P1:   *Have you got a red blouse?*
P2:   *Yes, I have.*
P1:   *Have you got a yellow skirt?*
P2:   *Yes, I have.*
P1:   *You're Lucy.*
8 (Extra) Transfer: Continue the 'Who is it?' game with the whole class, e.g. One pupil thinks of any other person in the room and secretly writes down their name. The others ask questions about this person's clothes (*Has she/he got a blue shirt/blouse?*) to try to identify the name of the person.

Reading and writing (ACTIVITY BOOK p.38)

9 **Activity ②** Pupils read the phrases describing the articles of clothing and their colours. They draw and colour the clothes in the empty frames accordingly.
10 **Activity ③** Pupils write the name of the article of clothing shown in each of the pictures. Remind them that they should write *a pair of...* for some of the clothing shown here.

Answers   1. a pair of shoes   3. a pair of socks
                2. a pair of jeans   4. a blouse

Ending the lesson

11 (Extra) If pupils have coloured pencils, play one or two rounds of Colours Bingo! Pupils draw a small colour 'flash' of any four of the eight colours they now know. Call out colour words, and play Bingo! as usual.

12 Play a few games of 'What can I see?', concentrating on the new clothes words and their spellings. Let pupils take over.

Be prepared!

Bring in the Feelie Bag and the alphabet letter-cards to the next lesson.

Lesson Three

Language focus
Revision: *Have you got...?* New vocabulary

New words
hat

Revision/Warm-up

1 Pupils work out anagrams of the new clothes words written on the board: *SESHO* (shoes), *TRISK* (skirt), *LUBOSE* (blouse), *SORTUSER* (trousers), *THRIS* (shirt).

Presentation/Revision

(PUPIL'S BOOK p.40, CS32)

2 *A question game.* This game revises recent vocabulary and the new colour adjectives.
 ● Play CS32: Ken and Caroline are playing the question game. Pupils listen and read the dialogue.
 ● Check that pupils understand how to play the game: One pupil secretly chooses one of the six strips of pictures without telling his or her partner. The partner must guess which strip has been chosen by asking *Have you got...?* questions and working out by elimination which strip it must be.

Practice

3 Pair work: Pupils play the game. Go round helping with vocabulary and pronunciation.

Reading and writing

(ACTIVITY BOOK pp.39-40)

4 AB p.39 **Activity** ④ Pupils say the words for each of the four pictures across the top:*t... telephone,**u...** umbrella, **w**...woman,**z**... zoo*. They listen especially to the sound of the initial letters of the four words.

● They then say the word for each of the pictures below and match its initial sound with its initial letter at the top, drawing a line to link the picture and the letter.

Answers   t - table, television (TV),
        trousers, telephone
    u - umbrella
    w - woman
    z - zoo

5 AB p.39 **Activity** ⑤ Pupils read the words in the box and circle only the clothes words.

Answers   trousers, skirt, coat, jeans, shoes,
    blouse, shirt, socks

6 AB p.40 **Activity** ⑥ Pre-teach the word *hat* with a sketch on the board and by mime.

● Pupils match each of the six sentences at the top with one of the pictures and write the letter for each picture in the appropriate box.

Answers   1.b   2.a   3.f   4.e   5.c   6.d

● Finally, pupils read the sentences and colour in the pictures as specified.

Ending the lesson

7 | (Extra) Anagrams race. Divide the class into two teams. Each team makes up an anagram from any recent family, animals, body or clothes words (or any other story words so far).

● The two teams write their anagrams on slips of paper, exchange papers and then race against each other to work out the correct spelling of each other's word. They score a point for correct spelling.

● Play two or three rounds.

8 | (Extra) Use the Feelie Bag and the alphabet letter-cards to have a spelling challenge game between two teams, as in Unit 5. Encourage pupils to think of and challenge their opponents with any recent new words. Let pupils take over as 'teacher'.

UNIT 11

Lesson One

Language focus
Parts of the body.

New words
arm foot / feet hand head knee leg shoulder toe touch (verb)

Revision/Warm-up

1 Play one or two rounds of the Spelling Shark with any new words from the last unit, especially the colour adjectives.

Presentation (PUPIL'S BOOK p.41)

2 *Head and shoulders.* Teach and then drill the new words shown on the picture of Zoko on PB p.41: touch your own arms, legs, shoulders, etc. as pupils listen and repeat.

● Ask *What's this?* as you point to the parts of the body, face and head again.Pupils answer.

● Pupils take turns to read out the words for the parts of the body on p.41. Help with pronunciation, especially the silent *k* in the word *knee*.

Song presentation

(PUPIL'S BOOK p.41, CS33)

3 *Knees and toes.* This is an 'action song'. Present the new song in the usual way, but get pupils to touch the parts of the body named in the song as they sing: e.g. touch hands to head... hands to shoulders... hands to knees... hands to toes... and repeat... etc. Encourage pupils to sing along with the tape.

● After singing: Point out that the word *foot* refers to one foot and that *feet* (in the song) refers to both feet together, as a pair. Do not yet focus attention otherwise on the regular plural form *-s*: it will be presented in Unit 12.

4 | (Extra) Dictation. Give a simple 'Picasso dictation', in which pupils listen and draw what they hear instead of writing it down word for word.
Demonstrate or explain the procedure to pupils. Then dictate each piece of the following description two or three times, giving pupils plenty of time to draw their pictures:

I'm a small monster./I've got a big head./I've got four eyes. /I've got a big mouth./I've got six long arms./I've got three small feet.../and I've got six big hands.

● Read through the description again slowly, section by section, letting pupils check that they have included all the right features in their drawings of the monster. All the pupils' drawings will of course be slightly different, but they should all have a similar number of eyes, arms, legs, etc. and of a similar size or length.

● Go over the dictation by drawing a monster picture on the board, feature by feature. Pupils check and correct their own.

Reading (ACTIVITY BOOK p.41)

5 **Activity ①** Pupils look at the body of the monster in the picture and then read the sentences. They decide whether the sentences are right or wrong and they circle the tick or cross accordingly.

Answers   1. ✓   3. ✓   5. x   7. x
           2. ✓   4. x   6. ✓   8. ✓

Ending the lesson

6 Play a game of 'Please and Thank you', using the instruction *Touch...* and the new parts of the body vocabulary. Demonstrate the meaning of the instruction by mime/gesture: e.g. *Touch your shoulder (please)... Touch your nose (please)... Touch your ear (please)... Touch your toes (please)*, etc.

Lesson Two

Language focus
Revision/Extension: recent new vocabulary

New words
I don't know.   *orange* (adjective)   *parrot*

Revision/Warm-up

1 Pupils sing the *Knees and toes* song, with actions and with CS33, if necessary.

2   (Extra) Play an anagrams game. Ask pupils to work out what these words are: *WOLLEY (yellow), NEERG (green),   EULB (blue),   DER (red).*

Story presentation

(PUPIL'S BOOK p.42, CS34)

3 *Can you see the balloons?* The story so far: Captain Shadow asked Woody and the twins to help her find Mr X again - his photo was in the newspaper. They went to the river and saw Mr X and his boat, but when Bean went to telephone Captain Shadow to tell her, Lifter caught him and drove him off in a big red car.

● Before listening: Pre-teach *I don't know*, using shrugged shoulders or other typical gestures to show its meaning. This can also become a useful piece of regular classroom language from now on.

● Set two simple questions now for pupils to think about as they listen and read:
a. What can Mr X hear?
b. Who is in Captain Shadow's aeroplane?

● Play CS34. Pupils listen and read.

● Play CS34 again. Pupils listen again and find the answers to the two questions.

● After listening: Choose pupils to give answers to the two set questions.

[Since texts are now becoming longer, stop using the 'listen and repeat' step of previous units.]

Story practice

4 Ask further questions orally about the story and pictures on PB p.42:
What colour is Lifter's hat? What colour are Bean's balloons? In Picture 2, what has Mr X got in his hand? In Picture 6, what can Captain Shadow see? What colour is Captain Shadow's coat? etc.

5 Dialogue: Pupils in pairs read and practise **Pictures 1 and 2 only** as a dialogue.

● One or two pairs act out the dialogue.

Presentation (PUPIL'S BOOK p.43, CS35)

6 *What colour is Kate's parrot?* Context: Kate's pet parrot has escaped from its cage. She is describing it to us so that we can help her to find it.
● Before listening: Pre-teach the word *parrot* (by pointing at one of the pictures at the top of PB p.43) and the new colour adjective *orange*. Drill the pronunciation.
● Play CS35. Pupils listen to Kate's description of her lost parrot and they look at the three 'photos'. They decide which of the three parrots must be Kate's, and they point to it.

Tapescript

Kate: Can you find my parrot, please?
He is a big bird. Here is a picture for you.
Can you see:
He's got a blue head... He's got a yellow nose... He's got a green coat... and red shoulders...
He's got orange legs and brown feet....
His name is 'Buttons'.
Look again, please: a blue head... a yellow nose... a green coat... red shoulders... orange legs and brown feet.

Answer Number 3.

Check the answer and play CS35 again if necessary, going through section by section.
● After listening: Ask a few questions about the three 'photos': e.g. *What has parrot number (2) got in his hand? What colour is his nose/head? What colour are his legs/toes?* etc.

Practice

7 (Extra) Pair work: Pupils take turns to choose any one of the three parrots at the top of PB p.43, without telling their partner which one it is. Their partner asks *Has he got...?* questions to find out which of the three parrots it is, identifying it by its picture number.

8 PB p.43 *Language puzzle.* Pupils follow the example, making properly ordered sentences from the jumbled words in the boxes. The sentences do not necessarily refer to any of the parrots above, but follow the same general theme.

Answers   1. What colour is your parrot?
2. Can you find Kate's parrot?
3. What colour is his nose?
4. He's got red shoulders.
5. His nose is orange.

Reading and writing (ACTIVITY BOOK p.42)

9 **Activity** ② Pupils colour in the picture of the parrot using colours they now know the names of in English.
● They then fill in the gaps in the sentences in Kate's speech bubble, using the appropriate colour adjectives.
● Alternatively, pupils could write colour adjectives into the gaps in the sentences first, and then colour in the parrot according to their chosen words.

10 **Activity** ③ Pupils choose a word from the box to complete each of the sentences below.

Answers   1. colour   3. What   5. red
2. got   4. trousers

Ending the lesson

11 Finish with the *Knees and toes* song, with actions.

Lesson Three

Language focus
Saying where people or things come from: *He's from (Africa).*
very + adjective: *very dangerous.*

New words
Africa England bad clever dangerous from very

Revision/Warm-up

1 Play a simple 'Draw, fold and pass' game, like this:
● Each pupil has a blank sheet of paper. Give an instruction: *Draw a head... Draw the nose, the eyes and the mouth.* Pupils draw a head with eyes, nose and mouth. They then fold over the top of their paper, to cover the head they have drawn, and pass on the paper to their neighbour.
● Give other instructions (*... the body,... the arms,... the hands,... the legs,... the knees,... the feet,... the toes*). Pupils draw, fold, and pass the paper to their neighbour each time.
● After drawing the feet, pupils unfold the whole drawing and individuals describe the one they have, using all the different adjectives they know: *She's got (a) big/small/long...etc.*

Reading (PUPIL'S BOOK p.44)

2 *Bob the Bad Banana.* Before reading: Remind pupils of the word *banana* and teach the new words *bad,* *dangerous, clever* and *very* by mime and gesture. Use a map of the world (sketched quickly on the board in outline, if necessary) to teach *Africa* and *England.* [An outline map is reproduced on p. 49 of this Teacher's Book.] Drill the pronunciation of the new words, as necessary. Finally teach *from* (a place), to describe where a person or thing comes from: point out that the B.B.B. is ***from** Africa* but that he is now ***in** England.*

● Pupils read the 'Wanted' poster either silently to themselves, or together in pairs, or aloud in turns, sentence by sentence round the class. Choose the best method to suit your particular class.

● After reading: Point out that *cannot* is the long form of *can't.*

● Ask the five comprehension question orally.

Answers   1. He's from Africa.
              2. He's got a red nose.
              3. Yes, his friend is dangerous.
              4. His coat is yellow and black.
              5. No, they can't.

Reading and writing

(ACTIVITY BOOK pp.43-4)

3 AB p.43 **Activity** ④ In this exercise, and those in the next few units, pupils are helped to see that written letters can make different sounds in English when they are read out.

● Here pupils look at two common ways to pronounce the letter *a:* the short /æ/ sound, as in *apple,* and the long /ɑ: / sound, as in *car.*

● Say the words *apple* and *car* several times, emphasizing how short or long the sound of the vowel *a* can be. Pupils listen and repeat.

● Now read the word *hand* from the box below. Say the words *apple* and *hand* together two or three times and indicate by facial expression and gesture that they are the same. Write them up together on the board.

● Pupils in turn continue to read words from the box in this way. Repeat each word read out together with either of the model words (*apple* or *car*), show by facial expression and gesture that they are the same or different, and then write the pairs of words with the same vowel sound up together on the board.

● Get pupils to decide if the vowel sounds in pairs of words are the same (e.g. *apple* and *hand*) or different (e.g. *car* and *hand*), and which group they should be written with. Two groups of words with the same sound will eventually be formed. Wipe these **from** the board.

● Ask pupils to write each word in the appropriate group in their books, according to the sound the letter *a* makes in each word.

Answers   apple - hand, happy, man, bank, family
              black, plan, map
              car - arm, father, party, are

4 AB p.43 **Activity** ⑤ Pupils complete the missing letters in the words.

Answers   1. newspaper   3. trousers
              2. head   4. hand

5 AB p.44 **Activity** ⑥ Pupils complete the crossword and find number 10 - *shoulders.*

Answers

¹E	A	R	¹⁰S			
			²H	E	A	D
		³N	O	S	E	
	⁴M	O	U	T	H	
			⁵L	E	G	S
⁶H	A	N	D	S		
	⁷K	N	E	E	S	
	⁸A	R	M	S		
⁹T	O	E	S			

6 AB p.44 **Activity** ⑦ Pupils read the sentences and write in *have* or *has,* as appropriate. Remind them in the last two examples that they should use a capital letter to begin a sentence.

Answers   1. has 2. has 3. have 4. Have 5. Has

Ending the lesson

7 (Extra) Game: The Whispering Race. Divide the class into two teams. Whisper any simple instruction to the first person in each team:
   - *Write the word **hippopotamus**.*
   - *Draw a parrot's face.*
   - *Stand up/Sit down.*
   - *Touch X's shoulder.*
   - *Find a yellow pencil.*
   ● The pupils in each team quickly whisper the instruction along the line from person to person. The last person in the team must do whatever the instruction says, as quickly as possible. The first team to finish correctly wins a point.
   ● The last pupil then moves up to the head of the line. Play another round using a different instruction. [Note: teams lose points for not whispering.]

UNIT 12

Lesson One

Language focus
Describing situations and scenes: *there is/are*.
Regular plural nouns: *-s*, *-es*.
Describing location: *in, on*.

New words
match   rabbit

Revision/Warm-up

1   Play the Please and Thank you game, using the instruction *Touch...* and parts of the body: *Touch your toes (please)... Touch George's arm (please)* etc.

Presentation (PUPIL'S BOOK p.45)

2   *There are five rabbits in the hat.* Context: PB p.45 (and also PB p.47) is based on the tricks of a clever magician with a magic wand and a magic hat. During the language presentation, dramatize the context with magician's gestures and some sense of suspense.

● Point at the top picture, the rabbit peeping out of the hat. Read the sentence twice: *There's one rabbit in the hat.* Pupils listen and repeat.

● Wave an imaginary magic wand over the book and point dramatically to the picture below as you also read the second sentence twice: *Now... there are five rabbits in the hat.*

● Drill the contrasted pronunciation of *one rabbit* and *five rabbits* several times, pointing at the drawings. Emphasize the pronunciation of the plural *rabbit**s*** especially.

● Repeat the same procedure for the magician's next two tricks: the bird/birds in the cage and the match/matches in the matchbox, waving the imaginary magic wand to dramatize each 'trick'. Again, emphasize and then drill the pronunciation of the plural *-s* or *-es* each time, as above.

● Point out the short form - long form linking of *there's* and *there is* in the usual way with a simple demonstration on the board.

● Point out also the three different ways in which the plural *-s* is pronounced in English. Start three lists of recent new words on the board.

(1) **'sss' sound**	(2) **'zzz' sound**	(3) **'izz' sound**
parrots	bananas	cages
coats	knees	matches

● Finally, specify the contrasted meaning of *in* and *on*. Pupils have met both these words informally before, but they can now be formalized. Give different contrasted examples, emphasized by gestures: *My book is **on** the table... My pen is **in** my bag*, etc.

Practice

3   (Extra) Listening game: Ask pupils to listen and repeat each of the following fifteen words two or three times after you. They then decide which list each one should go in, according to the sound of its plural *-s* or *-es*:

friends (2), *bosses* (3), *hands* (2), *maps* (1), *comics* (1), *blouses* (3), *newspapers* (2), *banks* (1), *matches* (3), *socks* (1), *shirts* (1), *toes* (2), *legs* (2), *oranges* (3), *boxes* (3).

4   A game: *Can you remember?* Pupils take turns to point at the objects in the picture at the bottom of p.45 and describe what they see there: *There's a parrot/ a big book/ a table/ one black pen/ one yellow ball/ an old man* and *There are two newspapers/ three balls/ two blue balls/ two red pens/ two blue pens/ two small boxes.*
Help especially with correct use of *There's* and *There are*, and with the plural *-s* sounds.

● Teach the meaning of the new word *remember* by giving examples and tapping your head: *How old are you, Mary? Ah yes, I remember! You're ten.* etc.

● Pair work: Pupils then close their books and take turns trying to describe the picture again accurately from memory, using *There's a ...* and *There are... .*

Reading and writing (ACTIVITY BOOK p.45)

5   **Activity ①** Pupils match the sentences with the pictures and write the identification letter of each picture in the appropriate box.

Answers   1.f 2.e 3.c 4.d 5.b 6.a

6   AB p.45 **Activity ②** Pupils write in *is* or *are* according to whether the object of the sentence is singular or plural in each case.

Answers   1. is ('s) 2. are 3. is ('s)
                   4. are 5. is ('s)

Ending the lesson

7 Play a few rounds of 'What can I see?', using objects (clothing, parts of the body, etc.) in the classroom. Let pupils take over the game as soon as possible.

Be prepared!

Bring the Feelie Bag to the next lesson.

Lesson Two

Language focus
Further practice of *there is/are*.
Asking about situations: *Is there...? Are there...?*

New words
corner follow I'm sorry   too (= also)

Revision/Warm-up

1 Play a game of 'Can you remember?' One by one put known objects of different (known) colours into the Feelie Bag. Pupils name them all together as you do so (e.g. *two green pencils, a yellow rubber, four red pencils, one ruler, five matches*, etc.).
● Pupils make sentences about what is in the bag, from memory: *There's one ruler in the bag. There are two green pencils.* etc. Help with vocabulary and pronunciation, as necessary.

Story presentation

(PUPIL'S BOOK p.46, CS36)

2 *Let's follow.* The story so far: Lifter and Mr X had kidnapped Bean but at the end of the last episode Captain Shadow had found Mr X's boat. While Mr X and Lifter were looking at Captain Shadow's aeroplane, Bean was able to escape and run away from the boat. Mr X decided that he was in danger, so now he has moved his boat to another part of the river, and has hidden it there... .
● Books closed. Before listening: Pre-teach only the new words *corner* (by a board sketch) and *follow* (by mime). Drill their pronunciation.
● Set two questions now for pupils to think about as they listen and read:
a. Can Mr X read the map? (Yes, he can.)
b. Can Lifter turn left at the corner? (No, she can't.)
● Play CS36. Pupils listen and read.

● Play CS36 again. Pupils find the answers to the two set questions.
● After listening: Individuals give answers to the two questions.
● Also ask pupils to work out the meaning of the words *I'm sorry* from their context or from the picture in Frame 4. This is obviously very useful social language and can become a regular part of pupils' classroom English from now on.

Story practice

3 Ask questions in English about the story and pictures on p.46: *Who is in the big car? What colour is Lifter's hat? What colour is Mr X's hat?*
4 Dialogue: Pupils in pairs read and practise **Picture 6 only** as a dialogue.
● One or two pairs act out the dialogue.

Presentation (PUPIL'S BOOK p.47)

5 *My uncle's hat.* Show pupils with board diagrams how the *Yes/No* question *Is there...?* is formed simply by inverting the statement form *There is...*:
There is a monkey in the bag.
Is there a monkey in the bag?
Also teach and drill the short answers to the question: *Yes, there is.* or *No, there isn't.*

Practice

6 Question-Answer: Pretend to be Kate's uncle, the magician. Ask one or two of the five questions about the picture of the magician and his hat at the top of p. 47. Help pupils with the required short answers, if necessary.
● Pair work: Pupils take turns pretending to be the magician and Kate, asking and answering the five questions about the picture, as at the top.
(Extra) Pupils could write short answers to the five questions at this point.

Answers	1. No, there isn't.	4. Yes, there is.
	2. Yes, there is.	5. Yes, there is.
	3. No, there isn't.	

Song presentation

(PUPIL'S BOOK p.47, CS37)

7 *Song - My uncle's hat.* Pre-teach the word *too (= also)* by giving examples of similar facts: *Mary is happy and George is happy too.*
● Play CS37. Present and practise the song in the usual way, encouraging pupils to sing along with the recording as soon as possible.

Reading and writing (ACTIVITY BOOK p.46)

8 Activity ③ Teach the question *Are there...?* and its short answer *Yes, there are.* Drill it several times by asking about objects in the classroom: *Are there pictures in your book?* etc.

● Pupils read the magician's speech bubble either silently to themselves, or aloud sentence by sentence in turn round the class. Remind them of the meaning of the word *map*.

● Pupils write *Yes, there is* or *Yes there are.* according to the form of the question, *Is there...?* or *Are there...?*

Answers
1. Yes, there is.	4. Yes, there is.
2. Yes, there are.	5. Yes, there are.
3. Yes, there is.	6. Yes, there is.

9 AB p.46 **Activity ④** Pupils give true answers: *Yes, there is* or *No, there isn't.*

Ending the lesson

10 Game. Have a Whispering Race with pupils in two teams as in the previous unit. Play three or four rounds.

Be prepared!

Bring the Feelie Bag to the next lesson also.

Lesson Three

Language focus
Revision of *can* + verb.

New words
animal duck America Asia Europe famous park play (verb) *walk* (verb)

Revision/Warm-up

1 Use the Feelie Bag and different (known) classroom objects, as at the beginning of the previous lesson. Pupils watch and name the objects as you put them into the bag. Get them to ask each other *Is there...?* and *Are there...?* questions about what is in the bag.

Reading (PUPIL'S BOOK p.48)

2 *London's parks.* This page is intended to revise and extend the use of *can* + verb as well as to give practice in reading comprehension.

● Before reading: Ask pupils to guess from the three photos on the page what the word *park* might mean and therefore what the whole passage here might be about. Help them with extra clues: e.g. name local parks. Also pre-teach the words *famous* (e.g. *Captain Shadow is a famous detective... Mr X is a famous robber*), *duck* (sketch or even mime!), and *walk* (by mime). Also teach the new names of continents (*Africa* is already known from the Bad Banana, p.44). Sketch an outline of the world on the board and label *America, Europe* and *Asia* on it in English. Drill the pronunciation of all the new words.

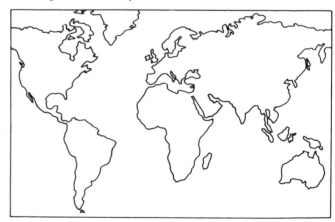

● Pupils read about the parks in London. They can read it silently to themselves or aloud sentence by sentence in turns round the class.

● After reading: Ask pupils to guess what the words *animals* and *play* (*football*) must mean from their contexts.

● Check that they understand the whole passage by asking simple *Yes/No* questions about it: *Are there three big parks in London? Is there a zoo in St James's Park? Is there a zoo in Regent's Park? Are there birds in London's zoo? Are there ducks in the parks?* etc.

● Pupils then read the seven statements below and decide if they are right or wrong. They circle either the tick or the cross accordingly.

Answers   1. x 2. x 3. ✓ 4. ✓ 5. ✓
6.and 7.(depends on pupil)

> ● (Extra) Very able classes or individuals could be asked to write short answers to the statements for extra homework.

Answers   1. No, there aren't.
2. No, it isn't.
3. Yes, there are.
4. Yes, you can.
5. Yes, you can.
6. (e.g. Yes, there are.)
7. (e.g. No, there isn't.)

Reading and writing

(ACTIVITY BOOK pp.47-8)

3 AB p.47 **Activity** ⑤ Follow the same presentation and demonstration steps here as those for step **3** of Unit 11, Lesson 3 (see p.46).

● Read out the two model words containing the letter *e*, at the top: *elephant* and *me*.

● Pupils repeat each model word two or three times after you, listening especially to the contrast of the *e* sounds.

● Pupils read out words from the box and decide which of the two different *e* sounds each word contains - is it like the *e* in *elephant* or the *e* in *me*? They then write each word in the appropriate group below, according to its *e* sound.

Answers   elephant - yes, desk, pen, red, letter,
yellow, clever, pencil, leg, left,
me - she, he, we

4 AB p.47 **Activity** ⑥ Pupils choose the appropriate word from the box to complete the sentences. Remind them that capital letters are used at the beginning of sentences in English.

Answers   1. are 2. there 3. Are 4. is 5. There

5 AB p.48 **Activity** ⑦ Pupils work their way through the maze from the top left to the river at the bottom right, completing and then following the ducks' directions.

Answers

6 AB p.48 **Activity** ⑧ Pupils read the words in the box and circle only animal or bird words.

Answers   rabbit, monkey, lion, dog, duck, parrot

[Note: *zoo* is a place and *cage* is an object. These two words are not themselves animal words, therefore.]

Ending the lesson

7 Sing any recent songs or chant any recent rhymes: *Knees and toes, the clothes rhyme, My uncle's hat,* or any other favourites. Use the relevant cassette section, if necessary.

Be prepared!

Bring in ten matchsticks to the next lesson.

UNIT 13

Lesson One

Language focus
Asking about number: *How many...?*

New words
bus

Revision/Warm-up

1 Start a Counting Chain round the class to revise numbers 1-10 (see p.20). Pupils who hesitate are 'out'.

2 Ask pupils to remember and chant the *Numbers rhyme* (Unit 3). Chant and clap the rhyme two or three times.

Presentation (PUPIL'S BOOK p.49, CS38)

3 Books closed. You need ten small objects, e.g. ten matches. Count the ten matches out on a desk. Pupils listen and repeat as you count. Ask *How many matches are there on the desk?*
● Take two matches away and ask the question again. Pupils answer: *eight*. Drill the question in this way, removing two or three matches, or putting one or two back again. Pupils listen and repeat the question together, before counting and answering.

Practice

4 Books closed. Play a simple game with the matches. Pupils in turn take over as 'teacher', asking the question and confirming or correcting the answers: *Yes, there are./No, there aren't. There are... matches.*

> ● (Extra) Turn this into a guessing game, hiding an unknown number of the matchsticks in each hand, holding out your closed hands and asking *How many matches have I got in this hand?... and in this hand?* Encourage pupils to *Guess!* Again let pupils ~~take~~ over as soon as possible.

5 PB p.49. *How many monsters are there?* Pre-teach and drill the word *bus*.
● Question - Answer: 'Spot the difference'. There are seven differences between the two pictures of children meeting space monsters. Use the PB p.49 in either of the following ways.

Option 1: Ask pupils questions about the detail in the two pictures: *How many girls are there? How many boys are there? How many buses are there? How many monsters are there? How many cars are there? How many arms have the monsters got in Picture 1? How many arms has the monster got in Picture 2? How many eyes...? What colour...?* etc.
Option 2: Get half the class to cover Picture 2 and look at Picture 1 only (Group 1), and the other half of the class to cover Picture 1 and look at Picture 2 only (Group 2). Ask pupils in Group 1:
　　　　T: *How many girls are there in Picture 1?*
Group 1 P: *Two.*
Then get pupils in Group 1 to ask the question to pupils in Group 2:
Group 1 P: *How many girls are there in Picture 2?*
Group 2 P: *Two.*
The two groups take turns to ask each other questions (as in Option 1, above) in this way, to find all the differences between the two pictures.

Answers　　Number of boys - two in Picture 1 and three in Picture 2.
Number of monsters - two in Picture 1 and one in Picture 2.
Number of bicycles - two in Picture 1 and one in Picture 2.
Number of cars - two in Picture 1 and one in Picture 2.
Number of buses - one in Picture 1 and two in Picture 2.
Number of arms on monster - three in Picture 1 and four in Picture 2.
Number of eyes on monster - four in Picture 1 and six in Picture 2.

● Pair work: Pupils take turns to choose either one of the two pictures of the children with the monsters from outer space, as Zoko and Kevin the hippo are doing in the example dialogue. Their partner asks *How many...?* questions about the pictures (as above) in order to find out which picture it must be.

6 PB p.49 CS38. Play CS38 now. Pupils listen to Zoko describing one of the pictures. They point to the right picture.

Tapescript

Zoko:　In this picture there are two girls. They've got blue jeans and yellow blouses. And I can see two cars and a bus. There are two monsters - they've got three arms and four eyes.

And there are two boys -
they've got blue jeans and green shirts.

Answer   Picture 1.

7 Transfer: Do a simple class survey. Ask pupils
   questions: *Who's got blue jeans/a yellow shirt/a
   green shirt/a bicycle/a computer/a big brother? Have
   you got a brother, Mary? And you, George?*
   ● Write up the results of the class survey in a
   simple chart:
   How many children have got a bicycle? six
   How many children have got a computer? two etc.
   [Note: Pupils only know the numbers to ten, so be
   sure to ask questions to which the answer will not
   be more than ten.]

8 (Extra) Game. Play a listening and counting game:
   ask pupils to close their eyes and listen. Tap the
   desk quickly but clearly with a pencil any number of
   times between one and ten, then ask *How many?*
   Pupils listen and answer. Let pupils take over the
   game.

Reading and writing (ACTIVITY BOOK p.49)

9 **Activity** ① Pupils read the questions below the
   picture and write full answers according to the
   details in the picture: *There are... in the picture.*

   Answers   1. Three   3. Seven   5. Four
                  2. Seven   4. Six

Ending the lesson

10 Pupils sing *My uncle's hat*, with CS37, if necessary.

Lesson Two

Language focus
Asking and answering about number (continued).

New words
at (a place) *basket a box of... chocolates hungry
idea in* (a street) *pizza rope shop street (St)
supermarket wait* (verb)

Revision/Warm-up

1 Play a guessing game with matchsticks, rubbers or
   pencils to revise the *How many...?* question form, as
   in the last lesson.

Story presentation

(PUPIL'S BOOK p.50, CS39)

2 *At the Supermarket.* The story so far: Mr X and Lifter
   have finally set off in their car to carry out their plan.
   On the way they have been spotted and followed by
   Poppy, Bean and Woody.
   ● Before listening: Pre-teach and drill the words
   street (and show the abbreviation *St* also),
   *supermarket, rope, pizza, a box of chocolates,
   basket, hungry* and *idea.* Use local examples
   (naming streets and supermarkets), sketches on the
   board, and mime, to present the meaning of the new
   words.
   ● Set two questions for pupils to think about as they
   listen and read:
   a. What has Mr X got in his basket in the
   supermarket? (A box of chocolates and a pizza.)
   b. Can Captain Shadow guess Mr X's plan? (Yes,
   she can.)
   ● Play CS39. Pupils listen and read.
   ● Play CS39 again. Pupils find the answers to the
   two questions.
   ● After listening: Ask pupils to guess from its
   context in Picture 5 what the word *wait* must mean.

Story practice

3 Ask further questions in English about the story and
   pictures on PB p.50: *What has (s)he got in her/his
   hand? What colour is/are...? Is there/Are there...?*
   etc.

4 Dialogue: Pupils in pairs read and practise **Pictures
   3 and 4 only** as a dialogue. They should take turns
   to be Captain Shadow here, since she has much
   more to say than Poppy.
   ● One or two pairs act out the dialogue, as usual.

5 | (Extra) Point out the phrases with *at...* and *in...* in Picture 1: *at* + name of a place in town (*the bank, a shop etc.*) and *in* + name of a town or street. Write some gapped sentences on the board for pupils to copy and complete by choosing *in* or *at*.
1. Poppy, Bean and Woody are ____ Main Street.
2. Mr X and Lifter are ____ the supermarket.
3. Let's wait ____ the Big City Bank.
4. The robbers are ____ London.

Presentation

(PUPIL'S BOOK p.51, CS40)

6 *Space City.* PB p.51 combines the space monster theme from PB p.49 with the names of some known places in town to give further practice of *How many...?* and of the preposition *in*.
● Pre-teach the words *shop* and (for recognition only) *space*. Drill the pronunciation. Also point out the word *street*, which pupils have only met in its abbreviated form before.
● Question - Answer: Ask *How many...?* questions about details in the picture. How many cars can you see in the picture? (2)   How many bicycles...? (1)
... monster dogs? (5)   ... blue monsters? (8)
... red monsters? (4)   ... green monsters? (6)
... yellow monsters? (8)   ... pink monsters? (2)
Help pupils to answer like Kate in the example:
I can see... .
● Pair work: Pupils take turns to ask and answer in the same way.

7 Play CS40. Pupils listen to the statements and look at the details of the picture on PB p.51 to decide whether the statements are right (*Yes*) or wrong (*No*), as in the example at the bottom of p. 51. Stop the tape when necessary to help pupils make correct answers.
● Play CS40 again.

Tapescript

Voice: There's a book shop in this street ...
           There's a book shop in this street.
Zoko: Yes, there is.
Voice: There are two yellow cars in the street ...
           There are two yellow cars in the street ...
Zoko: No, there aren't.
Voice: There are five bicycles in the street ...
           There are five bicycles in the street ...*
           [pause for pupils to answer]
Voice: There's a computer shop in the street ...
           There's a computer shop in the street ...*
Voice: There are two banks in the street ...
           There are two banks in the street ...*

Voice: There's a green car in the street ....
           There's a green car in the street ....*
Voice: There are four red dogs in the street ....
           There are four red dogs in the street .... *

Answers   1. No, (there aren't).
              2. Yes, (there is).
              3. No, (there aren't).
              4. No, (there isn't).
              5. Yes, (there are).

Reading and writing (ACTIVITY BOOK p.50)

8 **Activity** ② Pupils read the questions and look at the picture to find the right answers. They write complete sentences.

Answers   1. I can see five apples.
              2. I can see one newspaper.
              3. I can see four pencils.
              4. I can see one hat.
              5. I can see two boxes of matches.
              6. I can see five envelopes.
              7. I can see three boxes of chocolates.

Ending the lesson

9 | (Extra) Game. Find my word. Pupils say and spell out the names of different places in town that they now know. Write them at random on the board.

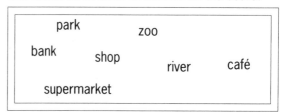

● Pair work: Pupil 1 silently chooses any word from the board and writes it on a slip of paper, folds it and gives it to 2. Pupil 2 asks questions: *Has the word got an A? Has it got a K?* etc. until it becomes clear which word Pupil 1 chose. They take turns and play several rounds.
● Finally ask the whole class to write out all the words in exact alphabetical order.

Be prepared!

Bring some coins or buttons (for counters in a game) to the next lesson.

Lesson Three

Language focus
Extending vocabulary for places in town.

New words
cinema eat film new problem restaurant take taxi

Revision/Warm-up

1 Play a few rounds of 'What can I see?' or 'Who is it?', and once pupils have guessed which object or person you have in mind, ask further questions: *How many... are there in this room? What colour is the...?* or *Has (George)... got a blue (shirt) today?* etc.

Reading (PUPIL'S BOOK p.52)

2 *Shops: A reading game.* Before reading: Pre-teach the new words for places in town: *restaurant, clothes shop* and *cinema* - name local examples of similar places. Also teach *eat* (by mime), *new* (show new clothes/books/pens etc.), and the words *film* and *taxi*.
Write the new words on the board and drill them.
● Demonstrate to pupils how the reading game works:
Get two pupils to come to the front of the class.
They read the START of the game aloud: *You are at the river.*
- One pupil flips a coin: the 'heads' side of the coin means 'GO'; the 'tails' side means 'STOP' (i.e. do not move on to the next section of the game). If the pupil's coin lands 'heads' side up, he or she can GO to the Bird's Cage Café, but if the coin lands 'tails' side up, he or she cannot move forward yet and must wait while the other pupil flips the coin and tries to get 'heads'.
- Pupils take turns to flip the coin, trying to move forward round the places in the city. When a pupil arrives at a new place, he or she stops and reads aloud what is written there. It is then their partner's turn to flip the coin.
- The first one to arrive at the Bank should stop and wait for the other person to catch up. They can then go to The Rex Cinema together.
● Pair work: Make sure that each pupil has a button or some small marker to move from section to section through the game, and that each pair of pupils has a coin to spin. Pupils play the reading game, taking turns to try to move forward to 'Finish' at the cinema, as described above. Go round helping pupils.

● After reading: Ask questions about the details of the pictures on PB p.52: *How many umbrellas are there at the cafe? Can you see a dog in the picture? What colour is the taxi/bus? What is the name of the cinema?*

Reading and writing

(ACTIVITY BOOK pp.51-2)

3 AB p.51 **Activity ③** Read the two words containing the letter *i*, at the top. Emphasize the different *i* sound: the short *i* in *hippo* and the long *i* in *icecream*.
● Pupils repeat each model word two or three times after you, listening especially to the contrast of the *i* sounds.
● Pupils read the words in the box to themselves. All the words are 'known' already by sight. They must decide which of the two different *i* sounds each word contains. They then write each word in the appropriate group below, according to the sound the letter *i* makes in each word.

Answers   hippo - in, comic, rabbit, this, cinema, twins, city
icecream - I'm, fine, hi, kite, right, bicycle, lion, white

4 AB p.51 **Activity ④** Pupils read and answer these 'transfer' questions.

Answers   1.Two.   2.Ten.
(Answers to 3, 4, 5 and 6. depend on the pupil).

5 AB p.52 **Activity ⑤** Pupils find and circle the words hidden in the letter square.
Answers

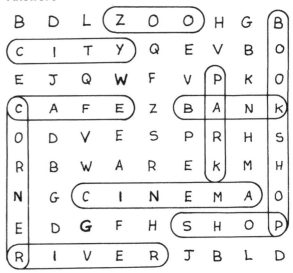

Ending the lesson

6 (Extra) Space City Game. Draw two circles to represent planets on diagonally opposite sides of the board: one at the bottom left and the other at top right. In the bottom left hand planet write *'WE ARE HERE'*, and in the top right hand one write *'SPACE CITY'*. Between the two draw a series of spaceship shapes, each big enough to write a word in.

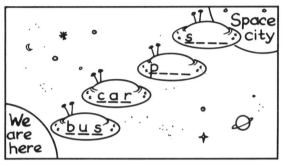

● The task is to complete the journey from *'HERE'* to *'SPACE CITY'* by correctly spelling a different word for each flying-saucer/spaceship. If the word is spelt correctly, it is written into the flying-saucer shape and another step on the journey has been completed. If it is not spelt correctly, it is not written in and pupils do not move forward on the journey. Use any recent new words as the words to be spelt: *shop, street, supermarket, cinema, restaurant, taxi* etc.
● This can be played as a game between two teams. For this, draw two sets of flying-saucer shapes between *'HERE'* and *'SPACE CITY'* and give different words to each of the teams in turn. The team which spells best will reach *'SPACE CITY'* first.

Be prepared!

Bring in **twelve** matchsticks to the next lesson, and a teaching clock, if you have one.

UNIT 14

Lesson One

Language focus

Clock times: (hours only) *What time is it? It's five o'clock.*

New words

eleven   twelve o'clock

Revision/Warm-up

1 (Extra) Ask pupils to work out what these anagrams of words from the last lesson are: *POSH (shop), ATIX (taxi), ZIPAZ (pizza), INACEM (cinema), PRASKERETUM (supermarket).*
● Let pupils play an anagrams team-game, swapping their anagrams and then racing to find the solutions, as before.

Presentation (PUPIL'S BOOK p.53, CS41)

2 Books closed. Use the twelve matchsticks to present the numbers *eleven* and *twelve*. Count the matches out onto the desk two or three times, as before, with pupils repeating the sequence of numbers after you. Drill *eleven* and *twelve*.
● Draw a clockface on the board, with numbers for each hour. Teach and drill the word *clock*.
● Draw the hands on the clock at three o'clock. Ask *What time is it?*, point to the clock hand at three and say *It's three o'clock.* Drill the question and the answer.
● Continue to drill all the hours from one to twelve o'clock in this way. Rub out the hour hand on the clock each time and draw it in again to show a different hour, asking *What time is it?* each time. Let pupils take over as 'teacher'.
[Note: if a teaching clock is available, use this instead of clockfaces drawn on the board.]

Practice

3 State a time: *It's five o'clock.* Pupils listen and hold up an appropriate number of fingers, indicating that time.

● (Extra) Game. One pupil has a piece of paper on which he or she draws a time on a clockface (hours o'clock only). The piece of paper is hidden from the other pupils . Then the pupil asks *What time is it?* and the others guess/ *It's one o'clock.* etc.

Practice (PB p.53 CS41)

4 *What time is it?* Ask pupils in turn to read and say the times on the five clockfaces at the top of PB p.53.
T: *Clock A. What time is it?*
P: *It's five o'clock.* etc.

5 CS41 Before listening: Explain to pupils that they will be using the five clockfaces across the top of the page to find what time it is in each of the four pictures in the bottom part of the page.
● Play CS41. Pupils listen and match each of the four statements on the tape with one of the four pictures. They then point to the clockface which shows the right time for each picture.
● Play CS41 again. Pupils listen again and check their answers.

Tapescript

Answers

Voice 1:	One.
Lion:	It's twelve o'clock.
	(pupils point to clock E)
Voice 1:	Two.
Kate and	
Ken:	It's nine o'clock. Come on. Let's go in.
	(pupils point to clock D)
Voice 1:	Three.
Lucy and	
Annie:	Can we play in the street, Mum? It's five o'clock.
	(pupils point to clock A)
Voice 1:	Four.
Clown:	It's eleven o'clock now.
	(pupils point to clock C)

(Don't forget to ask pupils to tell you the real time throughout the next few lessons at any time exactly on the hour. This will transfer the new language to real practical usage.)

6 | (Extra) Game: Time Race. Draw two large clockfaces without hands on the board. Divide the class into two teams.
● Call out times (*It's... o'clock*). The first two pupils in each team race to draw the hands on their clockface correctly. Each member of both teams has a turn. Keep scores.

Reading and writing (ACTIVITY BOOK p.53)

**7 Activity ① Pupils write the time shown on each

clock.

Answers   1. It's seven o'clock.
               2. It's four o'clock.
               3. It's ten o'clock.
               4. It's eight o'clock.
               5. It's one o'clock.
               6. It's eleven o'clock.
               7. It's five o'clock.
               8. It's twelve o'clock.

Ending the lesson

8 | (Extra) Clocks Bingo! Pupils draw six clockfaces showing different times (hours only) from one to twelve o'clock. They cross off their clocks as the hour is called out.

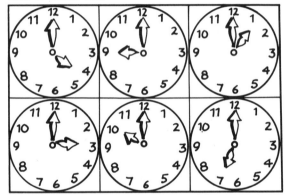

9 | (Extra) Spelling quiz. Divide the class into two teams. Teams take turns to challenge each other to spell any word they all know so far, without looking at their books. Each member of the asking team should think of one word to ask, but any member of the answering team may answer.

Be prepared!

Bring the Feelie Bag to the next lesson.

Lesson Two

Language focus

Practising telling the time. Specifying the time of day: *at six o'clock... in the evening.*

New words

bed bring evening get up Good night late money pretty put

Revision/Warm-up

1 Draw a clockface on the board and ask *What's the time?* each time you change the position of the hour hand. Pupils answer: *Its... o'clock.*

Story presentation

(PUPIL'S BOOK p.54, CS42)

2 *Banana Icecream.* The story so far: Mr X and Lifter went to a supermarket near the Big City Bank. They bought a box of chocolates, a pizza and a colourful skipping rope (which Lifter likes especially). Then they went back to their big red car, just near the bank... .
● Before listening: Pre-teach *bring, put* (by mime and gestures) and *money* (show some coins and notes). Drill the pronunciation of the new words.
● Set two questions for pupils to answer as they listen and read:
a. What time is it in Picture 2? (ten o'clock) And in Picture 6? (eleven o'clock)
b. What has Woody got in his hands in Picture 7? (the banana icecream)
● Play CS42. Pupils listen and read.
● Play CS42. Pupils listen again and find the answers to the two questions.
● Ask pupils to guess the meaning of the word *pretty* from its context in Picture 3 and from the picture.

Story practice

3 Ask further questions in English about the story and pictures on p.54: *Is/Are there...? Can you see a...? What colour is the...? Who has got a... in her hand?* etc.
4 Dialogue: Pupils in pairs read and practise **Pictures 2 and 3 only** as a dialogue.
● One or two pairs act out the dialogue, as usual.

Song presentation

(PUPIL'S BOOK p.55, CS43)

5 *The clock song.* Pre-teach *Get up!* (with gestures

and mime), *(It's) late* (mime), *Good night* (mime) and *bed* (sketch on the board). Drill the pronunciation of the new words and phrases, as necessary.
● Present and practise the song, playing the tape two or three times. Encourage pupils to sing along.
● Teach the use and meaning of the time phrases *in the morning* and *in the evening* by giving examples: *It's seven o'clock in the evening - let's watch TV.* etc.

Practice (PUPIL'S BOOK p.55)

6 *Language puzzle.* Pupils read the time statements on the left and match each one with one of the clockfaces on the right.

Answers

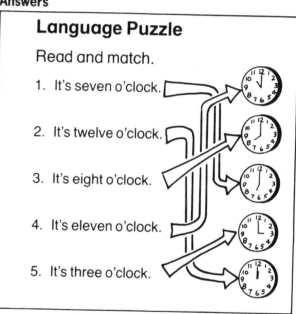

Language Puzzle

Read and match.

1. It's seven o'clock.
2. It's twelve o'clock.
3. It's eight o'clock.
4. It's eleven o'clock.
5. It's three o'clock.

Reading and writing

(ACTIVITY BOOK p.54)

7 **Activity ②** Teach the use of *at (... o'clock)* to specify an exact time - give the example from the story episode of this unit (PB p.54): *At eleven o'clock, come to the bank.*
● Pupils then follow tangled lines from each of the speech bubbles on the left to one of the clockfaces on the right to find out how to fill in the gaps in the speech bubbles.

Answers 1. Come to the café at four o'clock.
2. My party is at one o'clock.
3. The shops are open at eleven o'clock.
4. It's nine o'clock.
5. Please be ready at two o'clock.
6. The film is at seven o'clock.

Ending the lesson

8 Sing *The clock song* again with CS43, if necessary.

9 (Extra) Revision. Pupils turn back to PB p.52 and play the reading game again in pairs or groups of four.

Lesson Three

Language focus
Revision: possessive -'s. Vocabulary.

Revision/Warm-up

1 Revise the singular possessive -'s. Collect several different pencils, books, rubbers, rulers from pupils. Put them in a pile on the table and ask:

T: *Whose (pen) is this?*
P: *It's my (pen).*
T: *Ah, it's (Mary's/George's) (pen).* etc.
● Pupils listen and repeat the final line each time.
● Write the names of the owners and the objects on the board: *Mary's pen, George's ruler*, etc.

Presentation (PUPIL'S BOOK p.56)

2 *A game: What's in your box?* Zoko and Kate demonstrate how to play the game. Zoko has marked in red a group of four squares on his paper. Kate cannot see Zoko's paper and she asks questions to find out what group of squares he has chosen. In this block Zoko has got: Poppy's photo, Woody's socks, Woody's bicycle and Lifter's letter.
● Read through the dialogue between Kate and Zoko. Kate asks *Have you got...?* questions to find exactly which block or row of four pictures Zoko has got. Pretend to be Zoko with the same block of four pictures. Get pupils to ask you *Have you got...?* questions, as Kate does.
[Note: pictures can be chosen in a block or in a horizontal or vertical row.]

Practice (PUPIL'S BOOK p.56)

3 Pair work: Pupils play the game two or three times, taking turns to choose and **secretly** write down a

sentence to describe the block or row of pictures they have chosen from the panel: *I've got... and... and... and...* . Once written down, pupils cannot change their choices half-way through. Their partner can ask a maximum of ten questions to find the pictures chosen. Go round helping as necessary.

Reading and writing

(ACTIVITY BOOK pp.55-6)

4 Activity ③ Read the two words containing the letter *o*, at the top . The *o* sound is different in each case: a short *o* sound in *orange* and a long *o* sound in *nose*.
● Pupils repeat each model word two or three times after you, listening especially to the contrast of the *o* sounds.
● Pupils read the words in the box to themselves. All the words are 'known' already by sight. They must decide which of the two different *o* sounds each word contains. They then write each word in the appropriate group below, according to the sound the letter *o* makes in each word.

Answers: orange - doll, dog, robber, box, monster, sorry, shop, chocolates
nose - old, OK, no, hippo, clothes, hello, envelope

5 AB p.55 **Activity** ④ Pupils read the words in the box and circle only the words which refer to places in the city/town.

Answers   cinema, restaurant, supermarket, park, street, zoo, shop, bank

6 AB p.56 **Activity** ⑤ Pupils quickly read the three film 'posters'. It is important that they do not try to understand every word - the language is deliberately slightly above their level, and only some information is relevant to the exercise.
● Pupils read the statements below the 'posters'. They decide whether or not the statements are true by looking back at the information in the 'posters', and they circle either a tick or a cross accordingly.

Answers   1. ✓ 2. ✓ 3.x 4. ✓ 5.x

Ending the lesson

7 (Extra) Play a few rounds of the Spelling Shark with new words for places in the city.

UNIT 15

Lesson One

Language focus

Talking about shape: *circle, square, triangle.*

Revision: Adjectives of colour. Preposition of place: *in.*
How many...? with plural nouns.
Places in town vocabulary.

New words

circle   square   triangle   grey

Revision/Warm-up

1 Pupils tell you the names of places in town that they
now know in English. Write them at random on the
board and drill the pronunciation of each as you do
so.

```
        shop            bank
  book           park
      computer              supermarket
        zoo          clothes
  cinema      café          river
         shop            shop
          restaurant
```

● Start a chain game, like this:
T: *In this city there's a bank.*
P1: *In this city there's a bank and there's a zoo.*
P2: *In this city there's a bank and there's a zoo, and
there are three supermarkets.* etc.
Each pupil in the chain repeats the list and adds a
new item at random from the board: the chain gets
longer and harder to remember exactly. Pupils are
'out' when they cannot remember the whole list or
its order correctly.

Presentation (PUPIL'S BOOK p.57, CS44)

2 *Zoko's pictures.* Context: Zoko has been trying his
hand at painting abstract paintings. Here he is
displaying the results and talking about one of them.

● Books closed. Before listening: Pre-teach the
words *circle*, *square* and *triangle* by drawing the
shapes on the board. Also teach *grey* by pointing to
grey objects or clothing in the classroom. Remind
pupils of the word *picture*, which they have heard
before and seen in rubrics, but not actively used.

Drill the pronunciation of all the new words.
● At random, point to the board sketches and ask *Is
this a circle or a square?* and *What's this?*
● Play CS44 right through. Zoko describes one of
the three paintings. Pupils listen.
● Play CS44 again. Pupils listen and this time
decide which picture Zoko is talking about. They
point to it.

Tapescript

Zoko:
Look at my pictures, please.
In this picture here, there's one big black triangle.
There are nine matches. There are four grey triangles
and five pink triangles. It's a very good picture, I think.

Answer Picture C.

Practice

3 After listening: Ask the six *How many...?* questions
below the pictures on PB p.57. Help pupils to find
the right answers - Paintings B and C are picture
puzzles, so the answers are not as straightforward
as they may at first seem.
● (Extra)With very able pupils the six questions
could be set as a written exercise.

Answers
1. There are **twelve** circles in the picture.
2. I can find **five** green circles.
3. I can see **nine** squares in the picture.
   (Note: Not '**five**'; **four** other, smaller
   squares are made up of the
   overlapping corners of the **five** main
   squares in the painting.)
4. I can find **ten** triangles.
   (Note: Not 'nine'; the whole painting is
   inside one big triangle, which encloses
   the nine small pink and grey triangles. It
   is also possible to find three more
   triangles, each made up of four of the
   small triangles!)
5. There are **five** pink triangles in the
   picture.
6. There are **four** grey triangles in the
   picture.

4 Game: Can you remember? Pupils close their
books.
● Divide pupils into two teams of 'detectives.'
Teams take turns to ask each other *How many...?*
questions about the pictures on PB p.57: e.g. *How
many orange circles/brown circles/yellow circles/*

green squares/red squares/matches, etc. are there in Picture A/B/C? Teams score points for both correct questions and correct answers.

5 Do a simple 'Picasso dictation'. Pupils listen and carry out the following instructions, each repeated two or three times with a pause in between each to allow pupils time to draw and write:
*Draw a (blue) circle... Write the word **balloon** in the circle.*
*Draw a (green) square... Write the word **box** on the square. ... Write the word **apples** in the square.*
*Draw a (red) triangle. ... Write the word **pink** at one corner of the triangle.*
● Pupils check their work as you repeat the instructions slowly and give a model drawing on the board.

Reading (PUPIL'S BOOK p.52)

6 (Extra) Revision: *Shops: A reading game.* Pair work: Pupils play the reading game as they did in Unit 13, but with a different partner, and this time they should simply race right to the 'Finish' at the cinema, without waiting for their partner to catch up at the bank.
● Go round asking questions: *What is the name of the film at the Rex Cinema? ('Mickey Mouse' or 'Rocky') Is there a yellow taxi at the book shop? (Yes, there is.) What can you see at the door of the supermarket? (A green bus.) Can you see a boat in the picture? (Yes, I can.) How many boys and girls are there at the cinema? (Six)* etc.

Reading and writing

(ACTIVITY BOOK p.57)

7 **Activity** ① Pupils read the statements and decide if they are right or wrong, by looking at the pictures. They circle either the tick or the cross accordingly.

Answers   1.✓ 2.x 3.✓ 4.✓ 5.x 6.x

Ending the lesson

8 Finish with a song or rhyme.

Lesson Two

Language focus
Grammar revision

New words
heavy   Help!

Revision/Warm-up

1 Play a few rounds of the Spelling Shark, using any recent new adjectives (*clever, dangerous, famous, pink, grey, hungry, new, late, pretty*).

Story presentation

(PUPIL'S BOOK p.58, CS45)

2 *Now, Woody!* The story so far: Mr X has explained to Lifter his plan to rob the Big City Bank. They have set off from the car to the bank with the chocolate box in which the money should be put... but Captain Shadow, Pluto and the three children are waiting for them at the bank. Woody has a big tub of banana icecream... .
● Before listening: Pre-teach the new word *heavy* by mime. Drill its pronunciation.
● Set two questions for pupils to answer as they listen and read:
a. Can Captain Shadow and the children catch Mr X? (Yes, they can.)
b. Who is 'heavy'? (Pluto)
● Play CS45. Pupils listen and read.
● Play CS45 again. Pupils listen and find the answers to the two questions.
● After listening: Ask pupils to guess from context and from the pictures what the word *Help!* must mean in Picture 5. Ask them why Lifter says, *I'm sorry, boss* and what THE END means.

Story practice

3 Ask further questions about the story and pictures on PB p.58: *Is Captain Shadow in the bank or in the street? Is the box of chocolates in Mr X's hands or in Lifter's hands in Picture 2? Are Poppy and Bean in the bank or in the street? What has Mr X got on his face in Picture 5? Who has got the rope in Picture 7? Has Mr X got the money in Picture 7?* etc.

(Extra) Set two or three such questions for pupils to answer in writing now or later, for homework.

4 Dialogue: Pupils in pairs read and practise **Picture 2 only** as a dialogue.
● One or two pairs act out the dialogue.

Revision (PUPIL'S BOOK p.59)

5 *Look again, please.* The four grammar boxes on PB p.59 provide a review of the main verb forms covered in *Chatterbox* Book 1. The page is intended as a 'springboard' from which pupils can go back into different parts of the book and revise key language by repeating certain activities, games, songs, etc.

● Go over the four sections of the page one by one, getting pupils to make sentences on the basis of the verb patterns and sentence models in the boxes, using their own ideas and words as much as possible. Provide cues and hints to help them wherever necessary. Stop and revise, as necessary.

Suggested exercises

Write the following jumbled sentences on the board for pupils to re-order:

1. | friend | | is | | . | | She | | Mr X's |

2. | . | | are | | famous | | They | | robbers |

3. | a | | ? | | good | | Is | | detective | | she |

4. | the | | at | | they | | ? | | Are | | supermarket |

5. | very | | . | | are | | Woody | | twins | | and | | the | | clever |

HAVE GOT. Ask pupils to draw a picture of their family and write short sentences to describe each person: *My (brother/sister/etc.) has got short hair,* etc.

CAN. Pupils write five sentences saying who or what they can see on PB p.59, e.g. *I can see a parrot. I can see a monkey. I can see Lucy. I can see Annie, I can see Zoko.* etc.

THERE IS.... THERE ARE... . Pupils write five sentences to describe what is on the teacher's table or one of the desks (e.g. four books, two pencils, a cassette, a bag, a newspaper, etc.)

(Extra) Look back at the pages suggested each time under the 'Check' heading, and repeat any suggested activities, as necessary and as time allows.

Reading and writing (ACTIVITY BOOK p.58)

6 Activity ② Pupils read the words at the top one by one. They decide which of three sets each word belongs to: animals, clothes, or parts of the body. They then write the word in the appropriate place.

(Extra) Ask pupils to arrange the words in each set into exact alphabetical order before they write them in.

Answers   Animals - duck, elephant, hippopotamus, lion, monkey, parrot, rabbit, snake
Clothes - blouse, coat, hat, jeans, shirt, shoe, skirt, socks, trousers
Parts of the body - eyes, face, hair, hands, head, knees, legs, mouth, nose, shoulders, toes

Ending the lesson

7 Play a few games of Clocks Bingo! and 'What can I see?'

Lesson Three

Language focus
Revision of key language through story review.
Revision of key language through songs.

Revision/Warm-up

1 Pupils chant the Number Rhyme (Unit 3) and the Clothes Rhyme (Unit 10), from memory.

Revision (PUPIL'S BOOK p.60, CS46)

2 *Are you a good detective?* This listening practice page is based on single pictures from the past story episodes, and on short extracts from the same cassette sections.

● Before listening: Explain to pupils that they will hear five extracts on the tape. They should point to the picture which goes with what they hear on the tape.

● Play CS46 right through once. Pause the recording after each tape extract and give pupils time to point to the right picture.

● Play CS46 again. Pupils check and correct their answers.

Answers   1. a   2. c   3. b   4. e   5. d

● (Extra) Get pupils to tell you (in their mother tongue) as much as they can remember about the whole story, from memory.

3 (Extra) Dictation: Use any of the short story extracts in CS46 as the basis for a dictation.

● Play the chosen extract piece by piece two or three times, giving pupils time to write down what they hear.

● Play it again to allow pupils to check their spelling. Pupils can swap and correct each other's work, looking back at the appropriate story page.

Reading and writing

(ACTIVITY BOOK pp.59-60)

4 AB p.59 **Activity③** Read the two words containing the letter **u**, at the top. The u sound is different in each of the two; the short sound **u** in *umbrella* and the long sound **u** as in *ruler*.

● Pupils repeat each model word two or three times after you, listening especially to the contrast of the **u** sounds.

● Pupils read the words in the box to themselves. All the words are 'known' already by sight. They must decide which of the two different **u** sounds each word contains. They then write each word in the appropriate group below, according to the sound the letter **u** makes in each word.

Answers umbrella - rubber, number, hungry, duck, uncle, up, Mum
ruler - blue, supermarket

5 AB p.59 **Activity④** Pupils write true answers.

Answers 1. My name is (Mary).
2. I'm (nine).
3. I'm (tall).
4. My hair is (black).
5. My eyes are (grey).

6 AB p.60 **Activity⑤** Pupils complete the crossword and find the answer to number 11.

Answers

¹C	O	¹¹R	N	E	R	
²C	I	N	E	M	A	
			³S	H	O	P
		⁴S	T	R	E	E	T
		⁵C	A	F	E	
		⁶B	U	S		
	⁷C	A	R			
		⁸P	A	R	K	
	⁹B	A	N	K		
		¹⁰T	A	X	I	

Ending the lesson

7 Songs. The final cassette section plays all the nine songs from the Pupil's Book.

● Write the names of the songs in order on the board:

1. *a... b... c.. d... (The Alphabet Song)*
2. *How are you?*
3. *Happy birthday to you!*
4. *The happy hippo*
5. *The family song*
6. *The zoo song*
7. *Knees and toes*
8. *My uncle's hat*
9. *The clock song*

● Pupils then vote for songs they want to sing, in order. You will end up with a 'Hit Parade' of songs in order of popularity. Sing each song as it is voted for, using the recording on the last section of the tape for each one as necessary.

Word list

(The number after the word indicates the unit in which pupils first use the word. AB indicates that the word appears in the Activity Book.)

a/an	3
aeroplane	4
Africa	11
afternoon	2
am	1
America	12
animal	12
apple	3
are	2
arm	11
Asia	12
at	13
auntie	8
bad	11
bag	2
ball	4
balloon	4
banana	11
bank	9
basket	13
bed	14
bicycle	4
big	6
bird	9
black	10
blouse	10
blue	10
boat	4
book	2
boss	8
box	6
boy	7
bring	14
brother	7
brown	11

bus	13
but	11
bye	5
café	5
cage	9
calculator	6
can	9
car	4
cassette	2
catch	9
chocolates	13
cinema	13
circle	15
city	9
clever	11
clothes	10
coat	10
colour	10
Come here!	6
Come in!	1
Come on!	5
comic	8
computer	4
corner	12
cousin	8
Dad	7
dangerous	11
desk	2
detective	6
dog	6
doll	4
draw	AB1
duck	1
ear	7
eat	13
eight	3
elephant	3
eleven	14
envelope	4
Europe	12

evening	14
eye	7
face	8
family	7
famous	12
fat	8
father	7
film	13
find	3
fine	2
five	3
follow	12
foot	11
football	4
four	3
friend	7
from	11
get up	14
giraffe	9
girl	7
give	11
go	7
good	2
Good morning	2
Good night	14
Goodbye	1
green	10
grey	15
hair	7
hand	11
Happy birthday!	4
happy	6
hat	12
have got	7
he	5
head	11
hear	9
heavy	15
Hello	1
Help!	15

her	5
Here!	2
Hi!	4
hippo(potamus)	5
his	5
How old are you?	3
How are you?	2
How many?	13
hungry	13
I	1
icecream	3
idea	13
I don't know	11
in	7
is	1
It's a	4
jeans	10
kite	4
knee	11
late	14
lazy	8
left	9
leg	11
let's	10
letter	7
lion	9
listen	1
little	AB7
long	7
look	2
man	8
map	9
match (verb)	1
match (noun)	12
me	5
meet	5

money	14
monkey	9
monster	AB7
morning	14
mother	7
mouth	7
Mum	7
my	1
name	1
new	13
newspaper	10
nine	3
no	1
nose	7
now	5
number	3
o'clock	14
of (box of...)	13
Oh!	2
OK	5
old	8
on	12
one	3
orange (noun)	3
orange (colour)	11
pair	10
park	12
parrot	11
party	4
pen	2
pencil	2
perhaps	9
photo(graph)	9
picture	15
pink	12
pizza	13
plan	9
play	12
Please	2
point	1

pretty	14
put	14
Quick!	9
quiet	2
rabbit	12
read	1
ready	8
red	10
remember	12
repeat	1
restaurant	13
right	9
Right!	7
river	5
robber	7
rope	13
rubber	2
ruler	2
sad	8
say	2
see	9
seven	3
she	5
shirt	10
shoe	10
shop	13
short	7
shoulder	11
show	10
sing	1
sister	7
Sit down!	2
six	3
skirt	10
small	6
snake	9
sock	10
song	6
sorry	12
square	15

Stand up!	2
Stop!	2
straight on	9
street	13
supermarket	13
table	2
tall	8
take	13
taxi	13
telephone	3
television	6
ten	3
Thank you	2
the	6
There is/are	12
they	8
thin	8
this	1
three	3
time	14
to	7
today	2
toe	11
triangle	15
trousers	10
turn	9
twelve	14
twins	3
two	3
umbrella	3
uncle	8
very	11
wait	13
walk	12
watch (verb)	10
we	3
Well done!	1
what's	1

white	10
who's	1
whose	9
woman	8
word	AB1
write	AB1
yellow	10
yes	1
you	2
young	8
your	1
zero	3
zoo	9

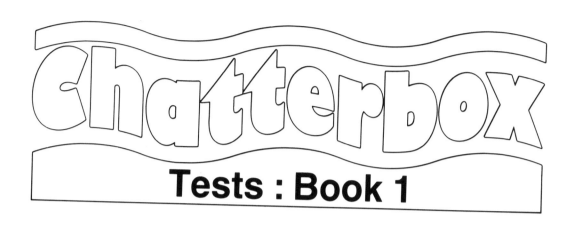

Tests : Book 1

Test 1   (Units 1–5)

What's this?   **Choose the right word.**   [5 marks]

Example :   an apple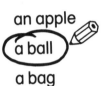
(a ball)
a bag

1   a pen
a boat
a pencil

2   a desk
an umbrella
a book

3   a bicycle
a car
a boat

4   a ball
a kite
a doll

5   an icecream
a rubber
an orange

Answer the questions.   [5 marks]

Example : What's this?

6 What's this?

7 What's this?

It's an orange.

_It's_ _____

_____

8 What's this?

9 What's this?

10 What's this?

_____   _____   _____

© Oxford University Press   Photocopiable

Read and match.   [5 marks]

a

Example : She's five.

b

Example : He's seven.

c

11 He's ten.

12 She's ten.

d

13 He's nine.

e

f

14 She's eight.

g

15 She's nine.

Complete the sentences.   **Write :** his **or** her.   [5 marks]

Example : It's __his__ bag.

Example : It's __her__ bicycle.

16 It's _____ ball.

17 It's _____ apple.

18 It's _____ balloon.

19 It's _____ icecream.

20 It's _____ book.

[**Total :** ___ marks out of 20]

Test 2   (Units 6–10)

Write : Yes, it is. **or** No, it isn't.   [5 marks]

Example :

Is it an elephant?

No, it isn't.

Is it a hippo?

Yes, it is.

3 Is it a doll?

_____

1 Is it a boat?

_____

4 Is it an envelope?

_____

2 Is it a snake?

_____

5 Is it a computer?

_____

Complete the sentences.   **Choose one word from the box.**   [5 marks]

short	ears	big	got	mouth

6 I've _____ small eyes.

7 I've got a _____ nose.

8 I've got _____ hair.

9 I've got a big _____ .

10 I've got small _____ .

I'm Mr X's friend. OK?

© Oxford University Press   Photocopiable

Read and match.   [5 marks]

Example : This monkey is happy. d

11 This monkey is thin. ☐

12 This monkey is sad. ☐

13 This monkey is old. ☐

14 This monkey is fat. ☐

15 This monkey is young. ☐

Read.   Colour Lifter's clothes.   [5 marks]

16 She's got a red skirt.

17 She's got a yellow blouse.

18 She's got white socks.

19 She's got black shoes.

20 She's got a green coat.

[Total : ____ marks out of 20]

Test 3 (Units 11–15)

Answer : right (√) or wrong (×). [5 marks]

Example :
The giraffe has got a long nose. √

1 The giraffe has got short legs. ☐

2 The hippo has got long legs. ☐

3 The monkey has got a big head. ☐

4 The monkey has got small hands. ☐

5 The giraffe has got small feet. ☐

Look at the picture.

Complete the sentences.   Choose words from the box.   [5 marks]

Example : There ____is____ a basket ____on____ the table.

6 There _____ four _____ on the table.

7 There _____ a _____ on the table.

8 There are _____ oranges in the _____.

9 _____ are _____ apples in the basket.

10 Is _____ a hat _____ the basket?

newspaper	~~on~~
There	basket
~~is~~	three	in
books	is	are
five	there

Write the answers.   [5 marks]

Example : How many boys can you see?   _Two_

11 How many buses can you see?   _____

12 How many monsters can you see?   _____

13 How many cars can you see?   _____

14 How many bicycles can you see?   _____

15 How many girls can you see?   _____

What time is it?   **Write the answers.**   [5 marks]

Example :   _It's two o'clock._

18

_____

16

_____

19

_____

17

_____

20

_____

[Total : ____ marks out of 20]

Note

The letter **e** occurs more frequently in written English than any other letter – **t** is next, then **a**, then **o**, and so on. The sequence of letters presented in this book for handwriting practice has been arranged in this order of 'frequency' – pupils first learn and practise letters they will need more often than others.

Find and colour the letters.

Write the letters.

e   e   e   e   e   e   e

t   t   t   t   t   t   t

a   a   a   a   a   a   a

o   o   o   o   o   o   o

n   n   n   n   n   n   n

r   r   r   r   r   r   r

i   i   i   i   i   i   i

s   s   s   s   s   s   s

Write the letters.

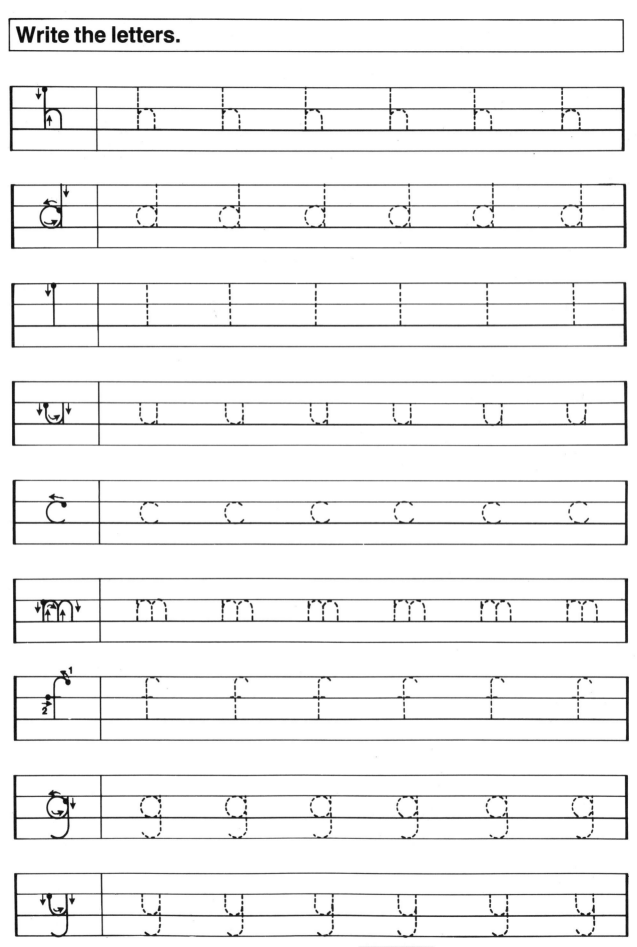

Write the letters.

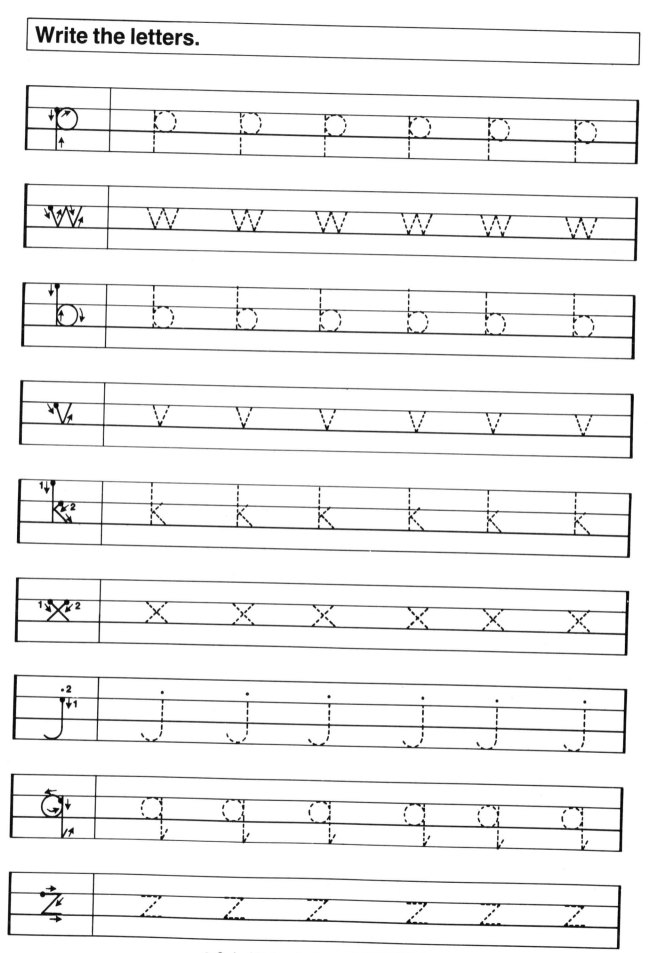

Read. Then colour the letters.

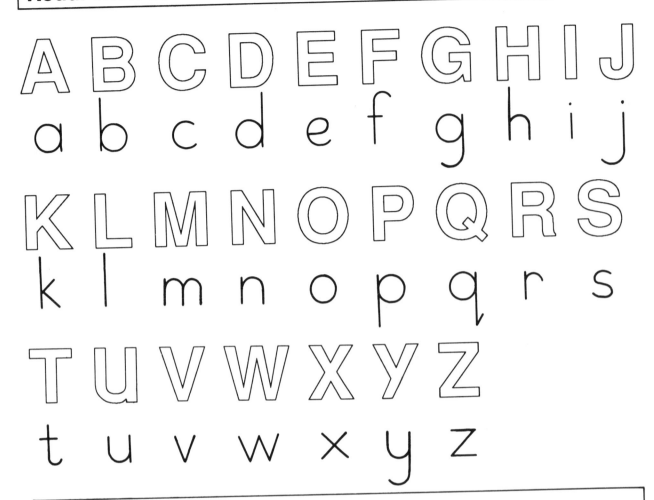

A B C D E F G H I J
a b c d e f g h i j

K L M N O P Q R S
k l m n o p q r s

T U V W X Y Z
t u v w x y z

Write the letters.

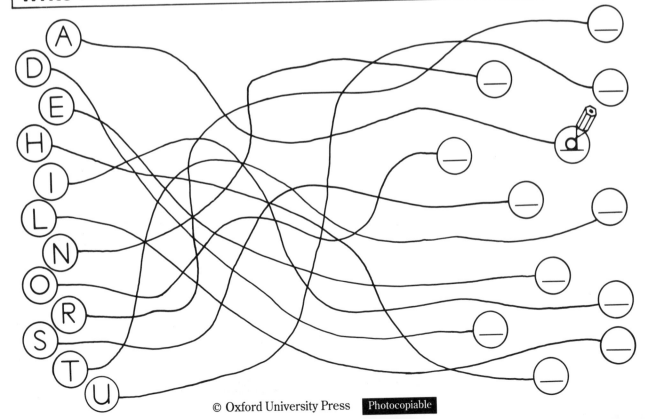

A
D
E
H
I
L
N
O
R
S
T
U

Write the letters.

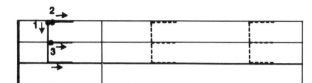

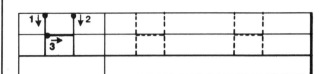

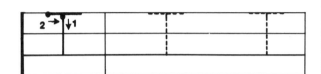

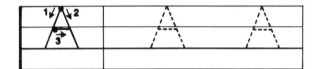

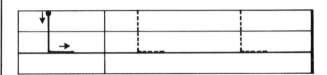

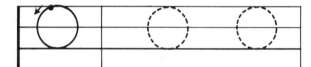

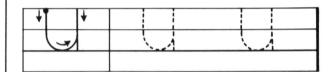

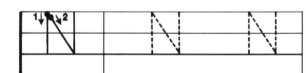

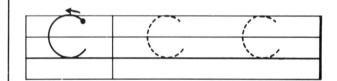

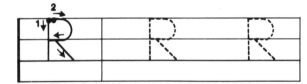

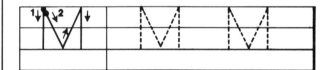

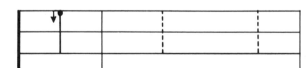

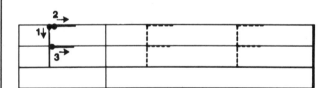

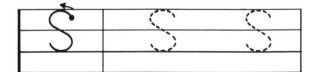

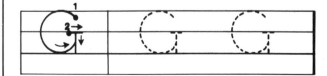

Write the letters.

Y Y Y
K K K
P P P
X X X
W W W
J J J
B B B
Q Q Q
V V V
Z Z Z

Write the letters.

A B C D E F G H I

J K L M N O P Q R

S T U V W X Y Z